My Grandfather's House

CHARLES RITCHIE

My Grandfather's House
SCENES OF CHILDHOOD AND YOUTH

Macmillan of Canada
A Division of Canada Publishing Corporation
Toronto, Ontario, Canada

Canadian Cataloguing in Publication Data
Ritchie, Charles, date.
 My grandfather's house

ISBN 0-7715-9512-3

1. Ritchie, Charles, date. - Childhood and
youth. 2. Diplomats - Canada - Biography.
I. Title.

FC561.R58A3 1987   327.2′092′4   C87-094158-5
F1034.R58A3 1987

Some of the names appearing in this book
have been altered, but all are those of real
persons not fictional characters.

Designed by Craig Allen

Edited by Patricia Kennedy

Copyedited by Eleanor Sinclair

Macmillan of Canada
A Division of Canada Publishing Corporation
Toronto, Ontario, Canada

Printed in Canada

*T*o the memory of my mother

"My Cousin Gerald" first appeared in
The Anthology Anthology, edited by Robert
Weaver and published by Macmillan of
Canada and CBC Enterprises, 1984.

Contents

ILLUSTRATIONS

Introduction

THE GROWN-UPS who surrounded us in childhood have a special place in our memories; they linger there long after many of our contemporaries are forgotten. Children see their elders in a strange half-light of their own—not at all as those elders see each other. Of course, their notions of people are influenced by their parents' opinions, but they often develop a positive passion for some unlikely person and take against a family friend.

When I look back on those distant figures who peopled my own childhood, I find myself increasingly curious about them. What were they really like? What were their stories? They were an oddly assorted company, ranging from my eccentric cousin Gerald to a dispossessed Russian princess, but for the most part their roots were in Halifax, Nova Scotia, where I myself grew up.

The city in the first quarter of the century looked backward towards its former prosperity. Among my mother's friends there were nostalgic tales of the old garrison days. My mother herself had an extraordinary gift for bringing the dead back to life in her talk, so that in my boyhood, echoes of the past were never far distant, and I did not feel too far away from an earlier Halifax, in which an older generation had lived. Theirs had been a small world, yet, small as it was, the currents of history run through all their stories. Not history as recorded in learned tomes or in the memoirs of statesmen, but history as it shaped the pattern of these different lives. From that day in August 1914 when, as a child playing on a beach, I heard of the outbreak of war, nothing was ever to be the same again—for me or for any of them.

I grew up in the aftermath of that war, in the uneasy interval of peace that followed. My memories of those years are of the friends of my youth. The scenes shift from the Halifax of my boyhood to London and Paris, to Oxford and Harvard. I was following the long trail of my education from one university to another, depending on such scholarships as I could pick up, supplemented by an allowance from my mother, which she could ill afford. I was in danger of becoming a perpetual student.

When, at intervals, I attempted to find work, I was none too successful. My brief encounter with journalism only served to prove that I was no journalist. My later spell of schoolmastering, that I was not a born teacher. How lucky I was finally to come to rest on the broad bosom of the Department of External Affairs!

My friends seemed as unsettled and footloose as I was myself. Perhaps more than we realized we were the creatures of the times in which we lived: Billy Coster, the witty American cosmopolitan who killed himself with drink—a tragedy of the twenties, with its atmosphere of frivolity and disillusionment; Julian Barrington, the communist son of Anglo Montreal—a product of the soul-searching of the Depression thirties.

There are few famous names among those appearing in these pages. For the most part they are long forgotten, like old photographs thrown out in a rummage sale, to which no one can now attach an identity. From this oblivion I have sought to rescue them, for why should the famous be the only ones to be remembered? I can only hope that my readers will find it a refreshing change to turn from the over-exposure of public faces to these pictures of private lives.

MY
GRANDFATHER'S
HOUSE

HE STREETS OF THE TOWN were steep as toboggan slides up to the granite Citadel and down to the harbour wharves. People were accustomed to walking on the perpendicular. The houses clung at odd angles to the spine of the hill, so that a roof or a protruding upper window showed out of alignment, as in a crooked drawing. The effect was disturbing to the sense of balance. The houses were of indeterminate age—some eighteenth-century, others Victorian, built of wood or stone beneath their coating of dun-coloured shingle. They were narrow houses, bigger than they looked from the front, with an air of reticence, almost of concealment. Nothing was for show. One sees such houses in Scottish towns. The poor lived in squat, bug-ridden wooden boxes, the windows sealed tight, winter and summer. A charnel whiff of ancient dirt issued from the doorways where the children thronged.

The Citadel crowned Halifax. It was flanked by army barracks built from London War Office blueprints, oblivious of climate or situation. Toy-sized cannon made a pretence of protection. Neat paths of painted white stones spaced with military precision and planted with a straggle of nasturtiums led to the officers' quarters. Barracks and brothels, the one could not live without the other. The brothels were at the foot of the hill near the waterfront and the naval dockyard. One could fancy that these rickety old structures would one day collapse from the vibration of the rutting that went on within their walls. From the wharves the stink of fish was wafted up the streets and the fog rolled in from the harbour, bringing with it a salty taste to the lips. The sound of the fog-horn was the warning melancholy music of the place.

Past my grandfather's house the trams rumbled, in front of it were three elm trees, behind it was a garden ending in abandoned stables. It was a tall, dark house. Inside, steep stairs went up and up; it made one gasp to look down from the top-floor landing into the hall-well far below. The stair banisters were narrow and dangerous to slide on. The house was lit by gas; pop! went the jets when lighted, and they gave off a pungent smell.

Each year my mother came to spend a winter month with her father in Halifax, and she brought me with her, first when I was six, then seven, then eight. My grandfather was a few years short of a hundred. When my mother was out shopping or visiting friends, I would be left playing with toys or reading in my grandfather's sitting-room while he fussed and fumbled about his desk. He was a small, cheerful, impatient man, with the white mutton-chop whiskers of another era, his hands mottled with brownish spots.

The sitting-room was hot and airless. Affixed to the panels of the door were strips of canvas on which bloomed sunflowers and lilies painted by my aunt Geraldine in an outburst of aestheticism in the 1890s. Over the mantelpiece were arranged photographs sepia with age. Some were groups of officers in which my uncle Harry figured boldly in his Highland uniform.

At times my grandfather seemed to have forgotten that I was in the room. The hours slid by unnoticed. Then, as though by a common impulse, we would both pause in what we were doing, he would subside with a sigh into his leather armchair before the fire, and I would break off my game or book. It was as though we were listening for something scarcely audible in the distance, but the only sounds were the shifting coals in the grate and the intermittent plashing of the snow as it slid from the window-panes to the ledge outside. Abruptly he would explode into talk: "When the Fenian raids threatened this country I led my boys into action. I charged up the hill waving my sword" (here, seizing the poker, he made to charge at me across the hearthrug) "and the Irish ruffians fled before us." My mother said that there was no charge and no hill, that my grandfather had raised a company to fight the Fenians but the raids were over before he could take to the field. I preferred my grandfather's version; his stories were like the stories I told myself or the games I invented. They were rambling and repetitious, and depended on the imagination.

When my mother came into the sitting-room, her cheeks flushed from the cold, she would fling off her sealskin coat and say, "Oh, how stuffy it is in here, what have you two been doing? Charlie, you ought to be out playing in the snow, it is a lovely sunny day. Father, you just have time for half an hour's rest before lunch."

There were many empty rooms in my grandfather's house, empty but furnished. The emptiest of all was my grandmother's bedroom, which had been left as it was when she was alive. The bed was made up; her hand-mirror, her hairbrush, and her Bible with a marker in it

[3]

were on the table beside her bed. No one but my grandfather was allowed to enter the room. Once I looked in and felt a breath of cold enclosed air on my face.

My grandfather's bedroom I visited every morning while he was still in bed in a flannel nightshirt, and he would give me a dusty lemon-drop out of a circular wooden box. The room smelled of old age—and of other things. He kept a ham and a bottle of stout under the bed, to conceal them from the doctor who had put him on a diet.

My grandfather had had twelve children. But he had outlived all of them but my mother and her brother Charlie. What had become of all those children? Most of them had died young, some in infancy, as so many used to in those days. Except for my mother, those who did grow up were not long-lived.

Of all the children who had played and called to each other in those rooms, two were to be met with at every turn. As soldiers they marched and countermarched along the garden paths, as Red Indians they put each other to the torture, as horses they galloped or trotted up and down to the stables. All their games and exploits were more real to me than my own. They were my mother and my uncle Charlie. These were the tales my mother told me, "Charlie and I, Charlie and I". He had been bold and adventurous; feats of nerve and truant defiance were his, and my mother had been his accomplice and his imitator.

What was he really like, Uncle Charlie? I still tease myself with the question. But he is nearly seventy years dead, killed leading his regiment at Bourlon Wood in 1918, against real enemies, not like my grandfather's phantom Fenians. The letters from the regiment after his death read, "The men would follow him anywhere; he seemed to bear a charmed life." Yet what was his life until the War gave him his chance? A life of adventure wearing down into plain middle-aged failure. Expelled from the Royal Military College for gambling, dismissed from the Mounted Police for striking a bullying corporal, disappearing for months into the Yukon, drifting into jobs and bars in Calgary or Edmonton, eking out his earnings by his gains at poker, he left a trail of legends and stories. A few old men still recount them, but his magnetism has evaporated and the point is gone.

His women were come-by-chance encounters doubled with romantic entanglements, for he had the attraction of the undomesticated man, restless and susceptible. He made husbands and other aspirants seem tame. The women who knew him felt they had a card up their sleeves. He never married. In a letter to my mother on the day before the battle in which he was killed, he wrote, "You are the only one I have ever loved." On the night that she was handed the telegram telling her of his death she saw, or thought she saw, him at her bedside. He wore a torn scarf knotted around his neck and there was a button missing on the left pocket of his tunic. Afterwards my mother wrote to the sergeant who had been with him when he was killed and he confirmed these details.

To my grandparents my uncle Charlie had always been a worry and a disappointment, sharpened by contrast with his elder brother Harry. Harry was their idol, a dashing soldier, startlingly handsome, cutting a figure in fashionable London, married to an Earl's daughter. But the idol was expensive to maintain. They paid his debts and waited for his letters, which came rarely—except when he needed money.

My grandparents were old-fashioned, innocent snobs. Innocent, in the sense that they never thought of themselves in this way. They believed that they had a Position to keep up (though what that Position was it would be hard to say). What made it more difficult to keep up was that my grandfather all his life drank in bursts of drunkenness, when he vanished from his wife and home for days at a time. My grandmother covered and concealed the outrage in the Victorian manner. Sometimes it was not easy. Once when she was presiding over a dinner party for some local dignitary, her husband, "unfortunately ill" upstairs, appeared at the dining-room door in his nightshirt, pleading for whisky. She rose from the table and majestically swept him away. He was smaller than she, and she so enveloped him in her amplitude that the guests could hardly believe, when she resumed her place, that he had ever been there.

Never in the course of nearly a century had my grandfather done a day's work. This, and his heavy drinking, may have accounted for his healthy old age. Although he was always prone to fits of gloom, his spirits revived quickly. The gloom was usually associated with money. He had inherited what used to be called "private means" from his father. Being generous and hospitable, he overspent his income. He and my grandmother found it difficult to retrench. My mother as a girl had no patience with their financial forebodings. "Why give dinner parties when we are in debt? Why import a spotty English boy and call him a footman?" My grandparents did not take these probings in good part. "Your father and I," my grandmother announced, "are pained, grieved, and disappointed in you, Lilian."

When I came to my grandfather's house as a child all this was long in the past. My grandmother's drawing-room was shuttered, its armchairs and sofas under dust-covers. The little papier-mâché chairs, almost too fragile to sit on, were pushed to the wall. The room was crowded with objects which seemed to me of inestimable rarity and strangeness. There was a picture of a boy in peasant costume holding an alpenstock; a souvenir from Switzerland, it was painted on cobweb. I held my breath when looking at it, believing that the picture would dissolve if I breathed on it. There was a silver horse trotting over a field of silver grass and flowers. In one corner of the room, enclosed in a large box, was a pile of old daguerreotypes. I would cautiously unfasten the rusty clasps of their black cases and bring to light a whole shadowy population. Men with fan-shaped whiskers and top hats, leaning gloomily against cardboard balus-trades, behind which hung a drop-curtain of majestic parks and castle towers out of proportion with watch-fob and frock-coat; women voluminously robed, bent pen-sively over a family album, one arm gracefully arched to support a languid head. All the denizens of this ghostly world wore the same expression of grave impassivity; even the children looked unnaturally solemn in their strange garb. They might have been the priests and priestesses of some fantastic and forgotten cult, the secret of which had perished with them. When I snapped the clasps of their cases to once again, it was as if I enclosed these dim beings in their tombs.

A marble group of the Three Graces stood on a red velvet pedestal under a glass case. Once when alone in the drawing-room I lifted the glass case with guiltily trembling hands and ran my fingers over the cold breasts of the Graces. I knew that I was committing sacrilege, but the desire for the unattainable was too strong for me to resist.

Over the drawing-room fireplace hung the portrait of a lady, her hair parted in the style of the Empress Eugénie, her dark eyes smiling, her pink scarf floating away from her shoulders into an azure sky. It was my grandmother. But not the stout old woman in a black silk dress whom I could just remember. This was she as a young bride, painted in Paris on her honeymoon in the 1850s.

Beyond the drawing-room was a small, damp library, also now disused. Here stood a desk, its drawers brimming with packets of letters yellowed by age, tied with faded ribbons. They were the letters of my great-grandfather to the girl he was to marry, written during their courtship. They folded inward on their broken seals of red wax. I unfolded them one after another. In one was a pressed mayflower that they had picked together in a wood. It was odourless and almost colourless. In another was a twist of hair, a living chestnut colour, leaving an oily stain upon the paper. The writing scrawled and hurried in haste or excitement, as though the nerves in the writer's hand were still alive. Bursts of feeling, scoldings, secret endearments, zigzagged across the pages. These letters were not meant for me. I was spying out of childish eyes.

Under the hall stairs swung a green baize door leading to the kitchen. Roxie was the cook. She had been with my grandparents all her grown-up life. She saw through them and she served them with cross-grained fidelity. She was red-haired and rough-tongued. When she finally retired to her family farm in Stewiacke, Nova Scotia, my brother and I used to spend a week with her there each year. She had no high opinion of me. "That there Charlie, when he is with you you would think butter would melt in his mouth, but just wait till your back is turned." They did not mince their words on the farm—"pee or get off the pot" was a favourite expression (and one which in later life I found to apply to many situations—social, political, and even amorous). Once when I returned from our annual visit my language surprised my mother. She was walking restlessly up and down in her bedroom smoking a cigarette when I suddenly said, "Why don't you sit down on your arse?" She came to a standstill, staring at me in disbelief. "What did you say?" "Well, that's what they say in Stewiacke." My mother was not genuinely shocked; she had little use for the genteel, and what she despised most, apart from cowardice, was what she called "affectation".

How far can one reach back into the past? Farther than the sound of a voice? My mother was a natural mimic. Her ear was a tuning-fork for voices and accents; the least actressy of women, she had a face as mobile as that of an actress. She could bring before you not only the absent, but also the dead—those whom she had known in her childhood. They might just have left the room, and one could catch the inflections of their voices, hear their laughter just before the door closed on them. So, I saw and heard those people of the past not as they might have been described in books, but in the flashes of her mimicry.

There was still a handful of survivors of my grandfather's generation living, among them Mr. and Mrs. Lorrimer. They were no favourites of my grandfather, particularly Mrs. Lorrimer, who had been a leading light in teetotal circles. She was one of the innumerable Queen Victorias who once peopled the Empire, modelling themselves on the Great Original. She had the lost Victorian art of putting one not at one's ease, but at one's unease. She dressed her part: a white cap perched on her severely parted white hair, and she was encased in an armature of whalebone. When she approached, there was a rustle of skirts, and the tap of her ivory-handled stick on the floor. She trundled rather than walked across a room; there appeared to be no leg action involved. She had a chilly little laugh, miles away from mirth.

The Lorrimers lived in the country not far out of town. I remember as a child going there once with my mother to lunch with them. We arrived somewhat late. "Dear Lilian," Mrs. Lorrimer greeted us with the little laugh. "I hear you were delayed by rain. How *very* extraordinary that we have had no rain here only a mile away, but it is no matter. Here you are at last." We went in to lunch preceded by a very old and smelly Newfoundland dog. Mrs. Lorrimer turned to my mother: "How is your father? Always so cheery. I am sorry your brother Charlie should be causing him so much concern. Your dear mother was always so indulgent to him, too much so, I fear." At that moment the dog growled and stirred under the table where he had crouched, and on a sharp note of rage my mother cried out "Damn!" There was a pause as if the clock had stopped. "He nipped my ankle," my mother explained. "Ha ha," guffawed Mr. Lorrimer, "she said a big D, she said a big D." Our hostess's laugh was like the rustling of dry leaves. "I am sure she said nothing of the kind, but if," turning to my mother, "you had said 'poor doggie' instead of the expression which you did employ, it would have been preferable." In front of my place at the table was a glass of milk. "We had it brought straight from the barn for you as a treat. It is warm from the cow." With revulsion I downed a swallow of the milk. It had a distastefully intimate taste.

The luncheon-table conversation continued. "So dreadfully sad," observed Mrs. Lorrimer, "for the poor

Brumleys that their only son should have become a pervert" (the reference was not to his sex preferences but to his conversion to the Roman Catholic Church), "but our own High Church so often leads the way to error." We rose to depart. "Dear Lilian," she said, "I remember you so well as a child and what a naughty little thing you were!" and, bending down to me, "Bonnie Prince Charlie, you didn't drink up your milk." A boy of six cannot suffer from the menopause, but my symptoms were those since described to me; a surge of heat flushed through my veins, and embarrassment dripped from me like sweat. Even today the words "Bonnie Prince Charlie" set up a queasy sensation in me as of the taste of warm milk.

My grandfather and his remaining contemporaries belonged to a breed now long extinct. They were Colonials. The word carries a whiff of inferiority, but they were not to know this. They thought of themselves as belonging to the British Empire, than which they could imagine nothing more glorious. They did not think of themselves as English. Certainly everything British was Best, but they viewed the individual Englishman with a critical eye. If the English patronized the Colonials, the Colonials sat in judgment on the English. The Colonial was an ambivalent creature, half in one element, half in another; British, but not English, cantankerously loyal. These were Nova Scotian Colonials. The earthy subsoil of Nova Scotia gave a tang to their personalities and an edge to their tongues. For many years they and those like them had managed the colony under the rule of British governors whom, in turn, they managed. It was a comfortable arrangement as long as it lasted, and not unprofitable. It enjoyed the blessings of the Church—the Church of England, of course. They were men of standing and standards, honourable men within the bounds of their monopoly. They were kind to their poor relations and moderately charitable to the poor who were not their relations and who lived in the slums. They began to think of themselves as an aristocracy, since there was no aristocracy on the spot to tell them differently. But they were small-town people, and they never escaped from the miasma of the small town. They woke to the apprehension of what the neighbours would say; they knew that, as always in Nova Scotia, ostentation was made to be undermined. There would be a dozen who would doubt the crests on their silver or the sources of their fortunes. So that they never achieved perfect complacency, a commodity hard to come by in that rocky land where misfortune revives friendship and where the worst word is "in trouble he let me down".

Halifax had been a garrison and a naval base for 150 years. Had not Kipling celebrated it as the "Warden of the honour of the North"? British regiments and sailors of the Royal Navy had come and gone in all those years and had set their stamp upon the town. No ball, picnic, or sleighing party was complete without them. They carried off the prettiest girls, and many a local man resented and hated them. They brought with them rumours of wars in the days when wars seemed an adventure, an honourable escape for the spirited and restless from home-grown tedium. Some found forgotten glory in those wars of Empire. Theirs were the tunes that went whistling up and down the steep hills of the town, "We're the soldiers of the Queen, my boys, the Queen, my boys, the Queen, my boys," and there were boys, like my uncles Harry and Charlie, to listen and serve.

When I came to my grandfather's house the British soldiers had marched down the streets for the last time and the little world in which my grandfather had grown up had long ago vanished. "I have lived too long, I have lived too long," he used to declaim in melodramatic tones. Yet all the sorrows and losses, the drinking, the fathering, the loving, and the talking (and he was a great talker) had not worn him out. He had been born in 1817 and was already a middle-aged man when Nova Scotia ceased to be a colony and became a province of Canada, an event that did not seem to have penetrated very far into his consciousness. He had never set foot in "Upper Canada", as he called it. His journeys had been those taken from Halifax to England, weeks spent in rolling, pitching, smelly little steamers, with shipwreck off the Grand Banks or Sable Island an accepted risk.

My grandfather never reached his hundredth year; he died ten days short of it. It was his impatience that killed him. Rather than waiting for help, he seized the heavy copper coal scuttle in his sitting-room and, in trying to pour the coal into the grate, he staggered, hit his head against the marble mantelpiece, and never recovered consciousness. My mother, my brother, and I were staying in the house at the time. By then it was 1917, and I was eleven years old. To me it was not the same house as it had been on my visits as a small child. I saw it with different and disparaging eyes.

On the day of my grandfather's death I was sent to the local cinema, I suppose to get me out of the way. When I went to bed that night in my bedroom at the top of the house I was not thinking of my grandfather. His death had not much moved me. He had come to seem no longer quite real to me, but like an old man on the stage who dies when the curtain falls.

At some moment in the night I woke to an intensity of listening. I got out of bed and stood at the top of the stairs, looking down to the gully where the banisters curved. The dense night silence reverberated around me; then there swept over me the tide of the past rising from the sleeping house below me. A constriction choked my throat. Had I heard a muffled sigh like a warning? What was it? Some signal from the frontier between childhood and old age where my grandfather and I had shared those timeless hours? When I went back to my bed it was to fall into a sleep as deep as the stairwell where the dead children had played.

MOLLY
CLARKE

MOLLY CLARKE was nineteen when she came out from Ireland to Nova Scotia to be my nursery governess. I was three years old at the time. Molly was the daughter of an impoverished Anglo-Irish clergyman. She was not regularly pretty, but she had a lovely complexion, bred in the rainy mists of County Kildare, and blue-grey eyes, and I fell in love with her on sight. For some years she was to be my constant companion, teaching me to read and write, getting me up in the morning, putting me to bed at night, taking me for walks and talking to me, for she was a great talker. I came to know her home and family like my own. She told me of her childhood, that she had always longed for adventure and to see the world away from the bleak village, from the dripping trees surrounding the Rectory, and from the family debts and squabbles. That was why she had taken the chance to come to Canada. She told me, too, of a girlhood romance with a boy in the village, a Roman Catholic not considered suitable by her parents, who, broken-hearted at losing her, had gone to be a soldier. Molly was a natural storyteller, and in me she had a perfect audience. I could listen for hours to that lilting Irish voice. Although she was romantic by nature she was no soft sentimentalist. She could be strict in her dealings with me and never coddled me. She despised what she called "muffishness", by which she meant all forms of holding back and timidity. What counted above all, she said, were loyalty and courage.

I thought Molly perfection. This view was not altogether shared by my parents, although they appreciated her good qualities and treated her as a member of the family. My mother thought that she talked too much and embroidered the truth, but she felt a sort of exasperated affection for her. They found it a great bore always having her with them at meals, and if my father was tired she was sometimes asked to take a tray to her own room.

About two years after she came to us, a young Halifax lawyer called Alec Thomson became a more and more frequent visitor to our house. He would sit in a corner of the drawing-room, usually in silence, gazing at Molly. Sometimes he and she would go for walks together. It was becoming obvious that he was a serious suitor. He was said to have excellent prospects at the bar, and came of a solidly well-to-do family. My parents encouraged this development. Alec was a small, sallow man. He spoke little, and when he did so was unable to pronounce the letter "r". Behind his back Molly used to mimic him, saying, "It's a vewy fine day fow a walk." But when he proposed to her she was undecided. I was outgrowing the need for a governess. She had no other training, and perhaps did not look forward to a lifetime of meals on trays. She had no desire to return to Ireland. Alec offered security.

Molly had a friend and admirer in my grandfather. She used often to go to tea with him and they would sit talking happily together. He welcomed her youthful company. She had a fondness for the warm-hearted, impulsive old man. My mother told me that Molly turned to him for advice. "I am not fascinated by Alec at all," she confided, "but what am I to do if I don't take him?" My grandfather was outraged at the idea. "It would be a sin and a shame," he said, "for a lovely young girl like you to marry a man she does not love." Molly agreed, and wept on his shoulder, but in the end she accepted Alec Thomson's proposal.

Her wedding took place in the Anglican Cathedral. She looked romantically youthful in my mother's wedding veil, but it was my own role in the ceremony which absorbed my attention. I was her page, to walk before her up the aisle. For the occasion I wore a suit of blue velvet with mother-of-pearl buttons. The other day I found a photograph of myself in this costume. I looked intensely pleased with my own appearance.

After their marriage, Alec and Molly moved to British Columbia, where prospects for a young lawyer were said to be bright. For Alec this did not prove to be the case. He moved from one law firm to another, from one locality to another, and my father heard through the legal network that he was not coming up to expectations. We did not lose touch with Molly. She wrote from time to time to my mother, putting a brave face on things and stoutly upholding Alec in his difficulties with clients and employers.

In 1912, we moved to Vancouver, but with the outbreak of war, my father joined the army. In the summer of 1915, my mother was in the midst of moving from Vancouver back to our home in Halifax. It was convenient to have me out of the way during the move, but what to do with me? A letter from Molly offered a solution. She suggested my coming to stay with Alec and her at Salmon Arm in British Columbia, where they were then living. She wrote enthusiastically of the beauties of the place, of Alec's successful practice, and of how much she looked forward to seeing "her dear little boy" again. The offer was welcome.

When I arrived in Salmon Arm, Molly greeted me like a long-lost son. (She and Alec had no children of their own.) Alec, for his part, accepted my presence with a kind of benevolent neutrality. He seemed even more silent and subdued than in the past. In the evenings, when I had been sent off to bed, Molly would come and sit beside me, talking to me as she had done at home. But now her thoughts ran on one subject—the War. Her two brothers were at the Front; one had been wounded, the other decorated for valour. She showed me their photographs, taken before they left for France, two very young-looking men standing stiffly in their new uniforms and smiling self-consciously at the camera.

I was a child of nine when I went to Salmon Arm. I do not remember when it was that I realized all was not well in the household there. It may have been the night when the electric lights went out. From one moment to another we were plunged in darkness. Molly called out to me, "Here is a candle, you can light it yourself. Isn't it fun, like in the old days you read about in your history books." The electricity never came on again. A few days later she was saying, "It's so much more peaceful without that blasted telephone ringing all the time." In fact, electricity and telephone had been cut off for non-payment of charges. Alec owed money all over Salmon Arm.

Molly used to take me with her into town on shopping expeditions. When she went into the butcher's or the grocer's she was met with glum looks. In return she overflowed with kindly inquiries: How were the grocer's children liking their new school?, How was the butcher's

wife's arthritis? She usually came away with her pur-
chases. "Put that down to my husband's account,
please," she would say. "He has been so busy with his
law practice that I am afraid he has been a tiny bit remiss
in settling that bill," and she sailed out of the shop. No
doubt the shopkeepers saw through her bluff. Perhaps
they admired her pluck and felt sorry for her.

Alec was not busy with his law practice. If he had an
office, he never appeared to go to it. He sat most of the
day in a small back room referred to as his study,
surrounded by law books, and smoking. Long afterwards I inquired from contemporaries as to the cause of
Alec's collapse in his profession. They said that he was
paralysingly shy in his appearances in court, negligent in
looking after his clients' interests, and a prickly, difficult
colleague. The truth was that, despite his self-effacing
manner, Alec had a rooted conviction of his own superiority. He could never understand why others whom he
considered inferior to himself succeeded. He brooded
over this injustice. Molly loyally backed him up in all his
quarrels and misfortunes. If she did not love him, she
obstinately believed in him.

All this I did not fully understand at the time, but I
sensed the cloud of debt and gloom hanging over the
house and saw Molly struggling to dispel it. Alec, for his
part, did not raise a finger to help her. I would hear her
brisk voice asking, "Alec dear, have you seen that
package of garden seeds?" and his monotone reply "No,
deawy." Only once when I was with them did Alec
emerge from his apathy. I remember the occasion.
When Molly and I came in from a walk we found him
sitting with a glass in his hand and a half-bottle of whisky
beside him. This was unusual; normally he drank little.
He was also in an unusually loquacious mood. Address-

ing me, he said, "When you grow up, remember that strong drink should never be taken in excess. Which reminds me of a Salvation Army song that I heard as a boy." At this he jumped up and, swaying slightly, began to sing in a high tuneless voice

Dwink Number One, only in fun,
Dwink Number Two, other boys do,
Dwink Number Twee, out on a spwee,
Dwink Number Four, just one dwink more,
Dwink Number Five, better look alive,
Dwink Number Six, bwains in a fix,
Dwink Number Seven, stars up in Heaven.

With that, he sat down hard on his chair and closed his eyes in sleep. Molly was not in the least disconcerted by this performance, simply saying, "Isn't it nice to see him so cheery?"

It was by accident that I discovered the one flaw in Alec which she could not forgive or, indeed, comprehend. I was in my upstairs bedroom one morning when I saw them walking together in the garden and, through the open windows, heard her voice. "Alec," she was saying, "you must go, for your own sake; you'll never forgive yourself if you don't. They need men at the Front now and you were in the militia, you have the army training." There ensued a silence, and the words "No, deawy." "Oh," she cried, in exasperation and near tears, "if I was a man I would go myself."

Alec never went to the war. What held him back? Not cowardice, I think; certainly not pacifist principles; perhaps it was sheer inertia, or an underground resistance to Molly's pressure. In the years that passed after my childhood visit to Salmon Arm my mother would receive bulletins from Molly. Alec had been accepted by a fine law firm in Victoria...Alec had had to resign from the firm due to the jealous interference of the senior partner...finally, Alec had died suddenly of heart failure. He had left Molly unexpectedly well off. In his last years he had inherited income from a family trust.

Molly went back to live in Salmon Arm. She wrote that she followed my diplomatic career and was proud of her boy. During the Second World War, when I was in London, she sent me a food package—tea, sugar, and chocolate, accompanied by a note reading, "I so envy you being in London during the air raids. They must be most thrilling." It was the last I heard of Molly until, shortly after the war, I received a lawyer's letter stating that I had been left a bequest under the will of the late Mrs. Alec Thomson. The bequest turned out to be a pair of Georgian silver candlesticks, engraved with the crest and motto of her Irish family. The motto read "Courage prevails". It seemed a fitting epitaph for Molly.

ON
LEAVE

OUR FAMILY was spending the month of August 1914 at Cohasset, on the coast of Washington State near Seattle. We were then living in Vancouver and it was an easy boat trip from Vancouver to Seattle. Cohasset consisted of little more than the small hotel in which we were staying and an expanse of beach on which my brother Roley and I were to play. I was seven years old in that summer. From the start I was bored with Cohasset. Children suffer from boredom more than one imagines, trailing listlessly about when they have played the same game over and over again and cannot think of a new one. The weather was hot and sticky. A dead whale had been beached on the sand, and its vast, putrefying bulk lay on the shoreline lapped by shallow waves. Above it, birds circled and dived, picking at the carcass. Some groups of mothers and nurses were scattered about the beach, talking among themselves but with an eye to the children playing in the surf. My own mother was one of these. It was a daily routine, but slowly I realized that this day was going to be different from all other days. I only half heard what the women about her were saying, "that terrible Kaiser", "war", and again, "war", but I knew

from the shocked, excited tones of their voices that
something extraordinary had happened. And there was
another note in these American voices, of awed sympa-
thy. My mother seemed singled out among them. "Of
course, you being British, it's different for you. Canada
will be at war, won't it?" So we were in some way special.
We were at war, *they* were not. People looked up as we
came into the hotel dining-room at lunch that day. I
found myself walking with a martial step.

Before the afternoon was out I had my private baptism
of fire. It was at the somnolent hour of three o'clock. The
grown-ups were resting in their rooms. Time hung
heavy. I sauntered into the drive in front of the hotel
where a patch of fading roses was wilting in the sun.
Beside the flower-bed was lying, half asleep, the handsome collie belonging to the son of the hotel proprietor, a
boy of my own age. I looked upon the dog as a friend. In
passing I gave him a patronizing pat on the head. The
collie sprang at my throat, there was a flash of fangs and
a smell of fur, and my left cheek was flapping, torn from
eye to mouth. There was a doctor staying in the hotel,
but there were no medical facilities nearer than Seattle.
The wound was cauterized with a red-hot poker—without anaesthetic. I was exhorted by the doctor to behave
"like a little man" and spare my mother's feelings. But I
howled unheroically. For years I kept my scar to remind
me of August 4, 1914.

On the outbreak of war, my father threw up his
practice as a lawyer and joined the army. In 1915 he was
appointed recruiting officer for the Maritime Provinces,
and we returned to Halifax to our home, The Bower. My
father pestered the military authorities to send him
overseas with the army. He told my mother that he could
no longer urge young men to join the army while he

himself stayed safe at home. His repeated requests were always denied. It was not surprising—he was fifty-five years old and partially deaf from the mastoid that was to kill him two years later.

In the hall at The Bower hung a map of the battlefields of the Front in France. Pins with miniature coloured flags attached to them marked the positions of the enemy and of the Allies. Every morning after reading the latest war news in the papers, my father altered the position of the pins to accord with the latest position of the opposing forces. I stood at his side as he attempted to outline the position at the Front. "Why," I kept on asking, "don't our flags move forward? They are just where they were last month. And look, in this place they've moved back." "That," my father patiently explained, "is what is called a tactical withdrawal." He was quoting the official war communiqués, but without conviction. The news was bad; he knew it and I knew that he knew it.

At the real Front, far from maps and pins, was my mother's beloved brother Charlie, in the thick of combat, the colonel of his regiment, wounded and decorated and returned to action. To us boys he was a hero. His Christmas card, stamped with the crest of the Princess Patricia's Light Infantry, was treasured by us as sacred. Then news came that put our household into a fever of expectation. Uncle Charlie was coming home to Halifax on leave from France. He would only be with us for a few days, but we would see our hero in the flesh.

He came to us straight from the trenches, and our settled home life must have seemed strange to him. His reality was elsewhere, and of that elsewhere he could tell us little. He did not talk of martial exploits, he had no words of hatred for the Hun, and what he did say sounded a wrong note in our ears. His stories of muddle and confusion in the High Command, his contempt for the red-tabbed staff officers, were like tales told out of school. Above all, it was his jokes which shocked ("Ha ha, that's when George got his head knocked off"), jokes that made broad comedy out of violent death, desperate jokes of fighting men that sounded meaninglessly callous to us.

But most of the time he tried to relearn the social charm and high spirits which had always been his. He tried hard with us boys, and was more successful with my five-year-old brother than with myself. Roley had the spontaneity of a small child; I was entering the stage of self-consciousness. Uncle Charlie spotted the difference at once. On his arrival he said, "Charlie gave me a peck on the cheek like an old married woman, but Roley kissed me like a lover." I smarted under the comparison.

The floor of one of the upper rooms in our house had been turned into a battleground. There we had deployed our armies of toy soldiers. The British, French, and Canadian forces were lined up on one side in battle array to face their German opponents. In front of the lines of infantry capered officers on horseback, bearing lances and paper flags. Toy cannon were grouped in artillery formation. No one but ourselves was allowed to touch the soldiers. When Uncle Charlie was shown this battleground he could not keep his hands off it. At once he began realigning the soldiers, scrapping the cavalry, talking of trenches and barbed wire, making a no man's land in the middle of the floor. It was like having a bigger boy joining in our game and upsetting everything.

Among my mother's women friends was my favourite, Aunt Lucy. She was an honorary aunt, no blood relation. She was beautiful. I knew that she was so because I had often heard it said by grown-ups. Children have no fixed notion of physical beauty. Sometimes, like lovers, they see those they love as beautiful in the face of the evidence.

Aunt Lucy was a widow. Before her marriage to a much older man, my uncle Charlie had been in love with her. She had been attracted to him, but he was then penniless and had a reputation for affairs with other women. His return on brief leave from the Front must have stirred the embers of this romance. Perhaps he had never forgotten a love which had escaped him, or he was making a last bid for happiness. Now she responded. She had never looked more lovely than in those few days when he was with us.

One evening, coming through the hall of the house, I saw that the door of the library, which always stood open, was closed. I was curious and pushed the door half-open. They were in each other's arms, two figures in embrace outlined against the open window. I had never before seen this melting of two bodies into each other. A breath of their physical passion reached me. Some rites were in progress from which I was excluded. Aunt Lucy in Uncle Charlie's arms was no longer my friend, but a stranger. I closed the library door and went up to my own room, disconsolate, mystified, yet stirred as by a premonition.

MY
UNCLE'S
MEDALS

IT WAS PARTLY A MATTER of economy and partly a matter of affection. We would let our house in Halifax, collect the rent, take ship for England, stay with my mother's aunt Zaidée in Cheltenham for the summer, and spend the winter on the Continent. My father had died the year before, leaving my mother a widow in her thirties. When we boarded the SS *Olympic* in June 1919, I was twelve and my brother, Roley, was four years younger. Rescued from a repulsive Nova Scotian boarding school, we boys saw this as an adventure. On the voyage over, I developed an irritating trick of chewing a piece of string and drawing it between my teeth. With a lurch of the ship, I swallowed it. When I told my mother of this accident, she said, "You foolish boy. It will twist itself around your entrails." For years afterwards, whenever I had a pain in my stomach I pictured the string doing its dire work.

My great-aunt's name had originally been Sadie, but she had embroidered it into Zaidée. The change never quite carried conviction, nor to me did my great-aunt herself. She was then in her eighties, but pretty was the only word for her, with her sparkling blue eyes, her "roseleaf" complexion, encouraged by touches of "roseleaf" rouge, and her soft little hands. On her finger she wore a ring composed of three bands of stones, each band the engagement ring presented to her by each of the three husbands she had outlived. The first, from the days of her Nova Scotian girlhood, was a gambler and a bankrupt; the second, a bishop; the third, a general. She trailed in velvet and smelled of the scent of Parma violets. She had a tinkling music-box laugh, and when she sneezed, it was as discreetly as a cat does. In her drawing-room, decapitated roses floated in silver bowls. She loved my mother, who had always been her favourite niece, and the love was returned, but we boys were rather too much for her. Me, she did not much care for. One reason for her carefully concealed distaste was my hay fever. Eyes oozing, nose dripping, convulsed by uncontrollable sneezing fits, I was not an attractive object, and my great-aunt preferred people and things to be decorative. When we drove out in her Victoria, I was encouraged to sit on the box next to the coachman to keep me out of sneezing distance, for her horses, like her roses, brought on an attack. I was happiest with the maids. She had four of them. On their days off, they would take Roley and me on bicycling expeditions as far as Gloucester or Worcester to visit cathedrals. We would sit with them for hours in the pantry, teasing and joking.

Our visit to Cheltenham was somewhat abruptly curtailed by an indiscretion of mine. I was in the habit of wandering into my great-aunt's sitting-room when she was absent. One day I saw an unfinished letter in her writing lying on her desk. Despite, or perhaps because of, the rule dinned into me that I must not read other people's letters, I picked it up. It read, "Dear Lilian and her boys are here on a visit. I expected them for a month and they have been here nearly two!" I reported this to my mother. She said that it was dishonourable on my part to have read the letter, but within a week we took our departure.

There followed a round of retaliatory visits to friends and relations who had stayed with us in Nova Scotia. By autumn, the supply of these began to dry up. My mother faced the problem of where we should go next. The answer came from an unexpected quarter, in the shape of a letter from Enid Leech-Proctor. She was the alleged fiancée of my mother's brother Charlie, who had been killed in action in the previous year, only a few days before the Armistice. After his death, my mother had heard from Miss Leech-Proctor, a name never mentioned to her by her brother. Her grief-stricken letter explained that she and my uncle were to have been married when the war was over. My mother, knowing her brother's propensity for getting involved with women and also his dexterity in getting himself uninvolved, was inclined to be sympathetic but sceptical. However, she wrote back warmly. Then came a proposal from Miss Leech-Proctor that we should spend a few months in Calais, where she was stationed in command of a Voluntary Aid Detachment camp on the outskirts of that town.

The idea attracted my mother for several reasons. In the first place, she was curious to meet her brother's fiancée; in the second, living in France was reported to be cheap; and in the third place, it would be an admirable opportunity for my brother and me to learn French. So, in December we embarked for Calais, rooms having been found for us in the town through a certain Major Beccles, a friend of Miss Leech-Proctor's. Although the war had been over for nearly a year, the British military were still in Calais, and accommodation could best be secured through them.

On our arrival, we were met by Major Beccles in person. He was a lean string of a man with a pot belly and a pipe, not at all my idea of a soldier. I think he had some kind of an administrative post connected to the leisurely evacuation of British army supplies from France. What I noticed particularly about him was that three buttons on the fly of his khaki breeches had been left unbuttoned, perhaps in his haste to be on hand to meet us at the boat.

He accompanied us in his military car to our new quarters, and on the way, his conversation was dispiriting. It consisted of warnings to my mother about the rapacity and chicanery of the French, and particularly of the inhabitants of Calais. When we arrived at our new home, it proved to be a red-brick house with steel shutters on the Quai du Rhin, overlooking a canal. The house belonged to a Monsieur and Madame Delfosse who inhabited the lower floors while our rooms were at the top. We were greeted by Madame Delfosse, a pouter pigeon of a woman with a fringe of dyed hair, who had at her heels a small yapping bitch. She showed us round our quarters. "Voici le petit salon," she said, throwing open the door on a minute sitting-room furnished with three chairs and a precarious-looking circular table inlaid with porcelain plaques. In addition, there were two bedrooms.

Miss Leech-Proctor's V.A.D. camp was situated across the sand dunes outside Calais, but she had military vehicles at her disposal and there were frequent exchanges of visits between us. She was a tall Englishwoman, and her V.A.D. uniform gave her an air both of military smartness and of dedication. Her abundant auburn hair was coiled under her service cap; her profile was noble; her eyes long-lashed and grey; her hands and feet exceptionally large. Between her and my mother, one of those hot-house friendships sprang up, nourished on shared loss and sorrow. In one emotional moment, my mother gave her my uncle's medals, her most cherished possession. She said that, as his future wife, she had the better right to them.

We had now begun to settle down to our life in Calais. It was necessary to find a tutor for Roley and myself, and here again Miss Leech-Proctor came to the rescue, recommending a youngish man recently demobilized from the British army, who was himself "polishing up" his French in Calais with the object of becoming a language master in an English preparatory school. He was a stocky, laconic man called Kenworthy, who seemed at first a strict taskmaster, but who proved easy to distract from our lessons if we could get him to talk about his war experiences. He was the son of the vicar of Miss Leech-Proctor's home town. She confided to my mother that at one time he had made some advances to her, but said that she had told him to "stop being such a silly boy and that one day the right girl would come along for him."

Calais proved to be a peculiarly sad, drab town, and there it seemed always to be raining, or about to rain, or just through raining. In the first flush of my enthusiasm, I used to set out on solitary walks, guidebook in hand, searching for monuments of the historic past. They were few and far between. In an ill-tended park, among the lifeless trees, stood a version of the Rodin statue of the brave Burghers of Calais with halters round their necks as they had appeared before King Edward of England offering to ransom their fellow citizens by their deaths.

They looked proud but dejected, and from their noses dripped the incessant Calais drizzle. My guidebook also mentioned as well worth a visit the Hôtel de Guise, where the scarred and sinister Duc de Guise of the Wars of Religion had once lived. After some hours of search, I found this dilapidated Renaissance building and penetrated into the courtyard. Its paving-stones were awash with liquid mud. Clotheslines stretched from hovels of tarpaulin and shingles which had been erected at angles from the main walls. From one of these dwellings issued an eldritch hag, who, pointing at the gate by which I had entered, began shouting unintelligible words at me in piercing tones of threat. Without actually running, I retreated pretty briskly into the street. That was the last I saw of the Hôtel de Guise.

But if the historic monuments of Calais proved disappointing, history was very much alive in the minds of its inhabitants, including those of Monsieur and Madame Delfosse, with whom I had now got on on such conversational terms as my French allowed. They were as anti-English as Major Beccles was anti-French. They wanted to know what the English were doing in Calais now that the war was over, and they thought they could guess the answer: Calais, in the past, had belonged to the English, and now they intended to take it back again. They had no intention of ever leaving. Their pretence of being concerned with the evacuation of British army stores was a transparent trick.

The Delfosses were not alone in their suspicions. During our stay at Quai du Rhin, the bodies of two British soldiers were found floating in the canal. Major Beccles believed that "the poor fellows had been knocked on the head by those damned Frenchmen." The Delfosses's version was that they had fallen into the canal while roistering with their drunken compatriots.

My mother inspired respect among the French because, like so many of the women of Calais in that year after the war, she was in widow's weeds. In her case, in mourning for my father. She also inspired interest of another kind. When we dined out in the neighbouring restaurant, Frenchmen at the tables around us gazed admiringly at this strikingly handsome woman with her magnificent dark eyes. From time to time, one would come over to our table and attempt conversation. Then my mother would say to me, "Talk. It doesn't matter what you say but keep on talking." This is a challenge I have always welcomed. While I talked, she would direct her gaze on me with unwonted attention. Her admirers would retreat out of respect for a devoted mother.

This was not the only intimation of desire that reached me in Calais. One day Roley and I, two small figures, were walking together rather disconsolately in the wastes of the sand dunes near the V.A.D. camp when we came upon a deserted casemate. On its walls were painted the insignia of the French regiment which had occupied it. To these, the French soldiers had added a series of drawings which had some of the vigour and muscular thrust of those to be seen in the Lascaux caves. Here was a frieze of sexual attitudes in which the organs of the actors were dramatically magnified and couples were depicted topsy-turvy, now on their haunches, now on their knees, now on their backs. I was riveted to the spot, trying to puzzle out exactly who was doing what with what to whom. The longer I gazed, the more hypnotized I became. Roley, four years younger, could not understand my interest and kept tugging on my arm to move on. But I was, for the first time, face to face with those Facts of Life of which I had heard only muffled rumours. So this was how it was done! And how many ways there were of doing it! Perhaps this first introduction to sexual love was not altogether fortunate. It gave me an awe-inspiring idea of the athletic achievement required for the operation. Later, when at Preparatory School in England I attempted to describe these scenes to other boys, one of them said to me in total disbelief, "I don't believe that King George and Queen Mary do things like that." This shook my confidence. I felt it improbable that those two crowned postage stamps would go through such convolutions.

The friendship between my mother and Miss Leech-Proctor appeared to grow even closer, yet it seemed to me, knowing my mother as I did, that a change was setting in. At the beginning, she had been drawn to Miss Leech-Proctor by her glowing looks, her emotional nature, and, above all, because she had been chosen by my uncle Charlie. The women whom he had loved had always had a fascination for her. Something of the magic with which she had endowed him seemed to her to attach to them. But as the weeks went by, I could detect warning signals that she was becoming bored, for Miss Leech-Proctor, alas, was both humourless and sentimental. While my mother still spoke of her with affection, she occasionally let drop a revealing aside, saying, for instance, "She walks like a policeman." It was true that when she strode over the sand dunes in her uniform, her large feet splayed out, she did have the look of a policeman walking his beat. On her side, however, a reverse process was at work. She was developing a romantic attachment to my mother and a tightening dependence on her. Perhaps she had discovered in her a streak of the same daring and impatient temperament that had drawn her to my uncle in the first place.

We boys found our visits to the camp a change from our cramped lodgings in the Quai du Rhin. There was always a warm welcome there for us from the ladies of the Voluntary Aid Detachment, who, anxious to fall in with their commandant's fancies, treated us as pets or camp mascots. The rough work at the camp was performed by German prisoners of war who for some reason had not yet been returned to their country. I have a memory of those blank-eyed figures with their shaven heads moving about the camp like zombies with slop-pails in their hands. When Roley and I played amateurish tennis together on the gritty camp tennis court, it was they who were detailed to collect the tennis balls that went astray and lob them back to us.

It was late autumn when we set out in one of Major Beccles's military cars in search of my uncle Charlie's grave. Miss Leech-Proctor's duties prevented her from accompanying us on this expedition. Under a blanket of cloud, we bumped along the shell-pitted roads and over the uneven cobblestones of ruined towns, and rain blew in gusts through the canvas flaps of the car. The scene about us was the stage-set of war from which the actors had departed. There was the authentic Flanders mud, miles upon miles of it; there were the bleached and blasted trees, protruding like toothpicks from the soil. Nothing living moved; even the dead had been stowed away; no human bones were left unburied; horses still lay where they had fallen, their skeleton rib-cages half embedded in furrows of mud, the bony structure of their eyeless heads gaping blindly at the eyeless sky. The litter of the battlefield was strewn everywhere: rusting weapons, burnt-out tanks, bandoleers of cartridges, mildewed leather belts, shreds of uniforms, and tin helmets. "Some people," said our army driver, "collect those

German helmets as kind of souvenirs." Immediately Roley and I set up the cry, "Can't we have some German helmets?" "What would you do with them?" my mother objected. "You don't want to drag them about with you the whole time you are in Europe and they would be so inconvenient to pack." But we persisted, and the car was stopped. Accompanied by the driver, we squelched across a sodden field, through which ran an abandoned trench. We gazed over its edge. On the floor of the trench, two rats of indecent size and sleekness were scuttling about.

It took longer than we thought to find the German helmets. Up to our knees in mire, we paused by a hollow tree trunk, out of which spilled a knapsack. It was stuffed with letters, some of which had fallen to the ground. The incomprehensible writing was in German and attached to one letter was the photograph of a young girl. Beside the tree trunk lay an unmistakable square German helmet. I seized on this, and a moment or two later the driver unearthed another. We returned to the car laden with the spoils of war.

On and on we drove while my mother struggled with the maps that Major Beccles had supplied. They were supposed to direct us to the military cemetery in which my uncle was buried. It grew darker. There was a confusion of roads in the half-light. When finally we found a Canadian cemetery, we wandered through avenues of crosses peering at the names, but his was not among them. On our return to the car, my mother, guided by what appeared to be a sudden intuition, said to the driver, "Turn left at the bottom of that road beside the poplar trees at the corner." He obeyed. Around the turn was a small plot of graves, which proved to be a temporary cemetery for soldiers of different nationalities awaiting transfer to their permanent burial places. There we found him. "Lieutenant-Colonel C. J. Stewart, D.S.O., Croix de Guerre". The name was on a little wooden cross. Roley and I removed our caps, bowed our heads self-consciously. Then we drove home through the night. On the way back, my mother was cross and tearless. She made no reference to the mysterious intuition which had caused her to direct the driver to her brother's grave.

As the autumn turned to winter, it was growing obvious that we could not spend the rest of our lives beside the canal in Calais. It was decided that we should join some family friends who were staying in a pension in Lausanne. Miss Leech-Proctor came to see us off at the station, and when she kissed my mother goodbye, her beautiful grey eyes filled with tears. En route to Switzerland, we stayed a few days in Paris, where Roley and I simultaneously developed chicken-pox. My mother thought that the hotel management would not allow us to stay on if they knew that we were suffering from a contagious disease. We were kept in bed, with instructions to cover our heads with sheets when the waiter or the hotel maid entered the bedroom so that our spots would not be seen. The waiter was certainly no spy. He was a frolicsome creature, the first male I had ever seen who painted his face and had his hair dyed gold. When we finally recovered enough to board the train, Roley and I discovered to our horror that our German helmets were missing. "What a pity," said my mother innocently. "We must have left them behind by mistake at the hotel."

We had not been long installed in the Pension Stucki in Lausanne when my mother received a letter from Miss Leech-Proctor announcing that she had a few weeks' leave from her duties and had the happy idea of paying us a visit. Great was our surprise, when she duly arrived in Lausanne, to find that she was accompanied by our former tutor, Mr. Kenworthy. "Poor boy," she explained. "He needed a holiday before taking up that horrid school-mastering job." In Switzerland, Miss Leech-Proctor seemed quite a different person from her Calais self. For one thing, she was out of uniform, and her uniform had seemed inseparable from her personality. Without it, she appeared to have lost height, not physically, but in some other fashion. In ordinary clothes, she looked more nearly ordinary. It was not only her appearance which had changed. She had adopted an almost skittish holiday manner which sat awkwardly on her. One day, as we were strolling through the town, she paused before a shop window filled with women's underclothes. "What divvy undies," she crooned, casting a mischievous glance at Mr. Kenworthy who was at her side. "Silly ass," I heard my mother mutter under her breath.

It was the boating accident that precipitated the breach. Mr. Kenworthy had hired a boat to go rowing on Lac Léman. The original plan had been to take Roley and me, but I had by this time had enough of Mr. Kenworthy's war memories and preferred to stay at home. Miss Leech-Proctor volunteered to go in my place. How the boat overturned was not at first clear. In any case, there was no great danger, as they were near shore and Mr. Kenworthy handily righted it again. They all got a soaking but returned to the pension none the worse for their adventure, except that Roley was shivering uncontrollably. "How," my mother asked him when Miss Leech-Proctor and Mr. Kenworthy had gone to a neighbouring bar for one of her favourite "white lady" cocktails, "How did they manage to upset the boat?"

"Well," Roley replied with artless candour, "they were kind of hugging and kissing each other and her hair came down and he was trying to put it up and somehow the boat went over on its side."

"I see," said my mother.

It was not long after that Miss Leech-Proctor departed from Lausanne before the end of her holiday. I was in the sitting-room of the pension, struggling with my French lesson, when she came to say goodbye. She arrived looking like a tragedy queen and carrying a small box in her hand. She went upstairs. From my mother's bed-room above, I could hear her tramping up and down with her policeman's tread. Only a murmur of voices was audible until the bedroom door opened and I heard Miss Leech-Proctor say in tearful tones, "But you are still fond of me, aren't you?" and my mother's resonant voice in reply, "No."

When I went up to join my mother, she was in a brisk and cheerful mood, apparently undisturbed by the scene she had been through. On the table by her bed was an open box. It contained my uncle's medals. "I asked her to return them to me," she said. "I don't believe he ever could have intended to marry her. She is such a bore and he couldn't stand bores."

With surprising pertinacity, Miss Leech-Proctor continued from time to time to send postcards to my mother giving news of herself. The last one came about a year later. It was a highly coloured view of Cyprus, announcing that she was on her honeymoon there. She mentioned the name of her husband; it was not Kenworthy.

IRINA

URING THE WINTER of 1919 my mother and we two boys, my brother Roley and I, were spending Christmas at the Pension Stucki in Lausanne. The table d'hôte at the pension seemed to shrink in quality and quantity week by week, but considering the cheapness of the pension rates we made no protest. Then one day at lunch, when the thin soup was followed by a one-egg omelette, a voice was raised in exasperation: "Do you think we can be feeding like little birds to pick at seeds!" The speaker was a woman, seated alone at the table next to our own, and her remark was addressed to the proprietress, Mme Stucki, who received it in silence, her mouth shut like a trap. After the speaker had left the dining-room, Mme Stucki remarked to us, "These Russians, they eat like horses. Just imagine to speak to me like that when she is behind in her payments. It is through charity that I keep her here. Before she was rich, now she is poor, but is that my fault?"

The Russian lady's name proved to be Irina Kirsanoff. Her room in the pension adjoined our own, and from casual encounters in the hall she and my mother struck up an acquaintance which quickly developed into friendship. Irina was then in her fifties. Her appearance was striking—grey hair piled in an untidy pyramid, high cheekbones ("I am pround of my Tartar descent"), a high-bridged nose with flaring nostrils, and the swinging gait of a cross-country walker. She was a vigorous and voluble woman, and we soon came to know a good deal about her. She was unmarried, came of a noble Russian family, and had escaped from the Revolution with her brother and his family, who now lived in Paris. She had had a summer property at Berchtesgaden in the Bavarian mountains which had been sequestrated by the Germans during the war, and she was engaged in an attempt to establish her ownership and to sell the property.

Irina's tales of her Russian past sounded strange and exotic to our ears. They poured forth in a disordered flood as she sat with my mother over endless cups of tea. It was my first exposure to that flow of Russian talk which slides from subject to subject, from the state of one's soul to the price of vegetables. At one moment Irina would be telling us of her great-aunt who lived in the days of serfdom. "When the Emperor Alexander II decreed the emancipation of the serfs, she was old and ill and could not get used to the notion that her household servants were no longer her serfs. As a girl she had known the Emperor. She wrote to him and told him of her plight. At one stroke of the pen he commanded that an exception be made. Her servants should remain serfs during her lifetime. That was noble gesture! In those days some families kept dwarfs as pets and playthings. My great-aunt had such a one, and she used sometimes to tease and pinch the little creature. I remember my father telling me that after her death the family was admitted to her bedroom where she was lying in state with candles lit about her body, and to their horror they saw the dwarf crouched on the bed over the dead woman, slapping her face over and over again—slap, slap, slap." Irina slapped the table vigorously in illustration. At other times she would tell of her own life: "I was lady-in-waiting to the late martyred Empress," she related. "Never have I known so shy a woman. When she had to give audience to some official she could not find a word to say and would go red in the face with embarrassment. Even though is was contrary to etiquette, I would myself sometimes intervene to help the conversation and to put her more at ease." My mother afterwards remarked that, judging by her own experience of conversing with Irina, she suspected that the Empress never had a chance to get a word in. Sometimes her conversation took a more personal turn. She would talk of love and passion, but she failed to draw my mother into any confidential exchanges on the subject. Once she surprised my mother by saying, "You Anglo-Saxon women are so cold. When I was younger, if I saw a man I fancied—a fine, well-built fellow, perhaps an instructor at the gymnasium where I did my exercises—I would say, 'Give me an hour of your time' and that was that."

My mother's health was not good during that winter. She had come down with a debilitating form of influenza. My brother and I were always in and out of her room. We were at a loose end, with no friends of our own age in Lausanne. My mother devised a plan to get us out of the way. Irina should take us in hand. She would teach us French (like most White Russian émigrés she was fluent in three or four languages); she would escort us on healthy walks, show us the sights of Lausanne, and keep us out of trouble. Irina welcomed the proposal—and the opportunity to earn a little much-needed money. The arrangement worked well. She turned out to be an ideal companion for children. She herself had the physical energy of a child and like many children was boastful and bossy. She never talked down to us but treated us as though we were her contemporaries. She took us for interminable walks in the hills near Lausanne. She said that if we had been with her at Berchtesgaden we could have climbed the mountains there. The Germans were the only non-Russians of whom she spoke with approval. As for the French and the English, they had betrayed the heroic White Russian general Denikin during the war against the Bolsheviks. The French cared only for money. "Imagine," she said. "I had a great friend, a certain French marquise. We have known each other since we were children. Last week I had a letter from her. She wrote, 'If you come to Paris, you will understand as a woman of the world that I cannot receive you as I would once have done as you are not in a position to reciprocate hospitality but I shall hope to see you privately from time to time.' A woman of the world!" Irina cried contemptuously, "Une femme du monde!" As for the English, "they have no souls. They are a nation of bourgeois. They imprisoned their great writer and poet, Oscar Wilde."

If the weather was too bad for walks, we three used sometimes to play a card game of Irina's invention. The cards were unlike any ordinary pack. They consisted of pasteboard reproductions of nineteenth-century Russian paintings. To each of these she had allotted a value; the highest—the equivalent of face cards—were battle scenes and historical episodes. Landscapes ranked lower. Pictures by artists particularly esteemed by Irina were trumps. You could take a trick with a Vassili

Verestchagin, a painter of dramatic scenes in Russian history, or a Repnin, who had painted a portrait of her grandmother. She herself was a highly competitive player who loved to win. If she lost, she suspected the worst. "You are hiding a card up your sleeve," she would cry. "Take your elbows off the table." Once, in a moment of excitement, she shouted at my small brother, "If you don't stop cheating I shall tie your hands under the chair!" We were not in the least intimidated by these threats, but we were taken aback at the accusation of cheating, which we had been taught to think the unforgivable sin.

Despite her despotic ways, we became very fond of Irina, and when the time came for us to return to school we felt we were parting from an old friend. Irina herself was leaving Lausanne to live with her brother, Prince Kirsanoff, and his family in Paris. We exchanged addresses and promises to write, but with scant prospects of meeting her again. We returned to school, our education enriched with some speaking knowledge of French with a strong Russian accent, a close acquaintance with Russian nineteenth-century painting, and the conviction that the English had no souls.

More than ten years passed before Irina came into my life again. We had never entirely lost touch with her; there had been exchanges of postcards. We learned that she was still living with her sister-in-law and her family in Paris, although her brother had died.

When in 1931 I myself went to Paris to continue my interminable education as a student at the École Libre des Sciences Politiques, my first thought was not of a reunion with Irina. Having just escaped from the rigours of a celibate existence in a post-graduate residence at Harvard, I was fully occupied in making up for lost time.

By great good fortune I had encountered a lively and spirited girl who had nothing better to do during a visit to Paris than to join me in this pursuit. There followed one of those brief interludes of unalloyed happiness that the gods occasionally allow us. Paris in fine September weather was the perfect backdrop for our idyll. We walked together along the quais by the Seine; we paused hand in hand before the statues of dead poets in the Luxembourg Gardens. We sat for hours at café tables in the Boulevard Saint-Germain, deep in talk or silently satisfied, like cats in the sun. We came back in the afternoon to closed shutters, cool darkness, and muffled murmurs. It was of course too good to last. The time came for her departure. We swore oaths of eternal fidelity, and once again I was left with time on my hands. Time but not money.

I had given little thought to money in the previous weeks. Now I took stock of my increasingly awkward situation. When I arrived in Paris I had taken a room at a small but expensive hotel in the rue Cambon, intending to stay there only a night or two while looking round for accommodation with a French family to improve my knowledge of the language. However, there had proved to be a compelling reason to have a room of my own away from family life. Meanwhile my weekly bills at the hotel had been accumulating. At the same time I was suffering from the loneliness and disarray that follow an interrupted love affair. I needed the comfort of an old friend. I turned to Irina.

When I arrived at the Kirsanoff family apartment in the Boulevard Haussmann, she was at the door to welcome me with a hug and a kiss. She seemed quite unchanged. It was as though we had parted the day before in the Pension Stucki. The hall of the Kirsanoffs' apartment was large and darkly panelled. On one side stood a long dining-room table. On the other I could dimly discern shadowy shapes which appeared to be busts of full-breasted women but were, as it turned out, tailors' dummies. When she saw me gazing at them with mystification, Irina explained, "It is my sister-in-law's dressmaking. She has many customers, American ladies for the most part. All of us in this family make ourselves useful. For my part, I am teaching French and German and I have good pupils; some are to be future diplomats and professors. My older nephew, Kirill, deals in antiques. My younger nephew, Ivan, drives a taxi. He is such a fine fellow, so simple and sincere. You and he must become friends. My niece, Natasha, is a student, very serious. But enough of me and my family. What are you doing in Paris?" When I explained that I too was a student, she said, "So now you are fluent in the French language?"

This was far from being the case. I was dependent on the rudiments remaining from my boyhood lessons with Irina herself and the bare bones of the language as taught in English and Canadian schools. I was already having some difficulty in following the lectures at the École. When I admitted this to her, she said, "You shall take French lessons from me. It will be like old times." It seemed a good idea. The lessons would be useful to me and the money would be useful to her, but it was obvious that I could not afford this additional expense while remaining at the hotel. When I explained the problem to Irina, she was again ready with an answer. "Of course you must not stay at a hotel. Russian friends of ours, the Schébékos, have a room in their flat which they let to students. At present it is empty. It is just the thing for you, not at all expensive. Madame Schébéko is a charming person, and her husband used to be our ambassador in Vienna before the Revolution. You can talk about diplomacy to him in French." So in the space of half an hour Irina had taken charge of my life. Within a few days I was installed at the Schébékos' and taking lessons with Irina three times a week.

The Schébékos' flat was in a quiet street in Neuilly. My bed-sitting room was large and comfortable. Madame Schébéko was friendly. Her charming, easy manner had been perfected in the drawing-rooms of pre-war St. Petersburg. Above the sofa in the sitting-room, salvaged from the Imperial Russian Embassy in Vienna, hung a portrait of her as a young and fashionable beauty. Now she served long hours behind the counter in a neighbouring Russian restaurant. "Before the Revolution," she once told me, "I saw a magnificent sable coat. I thought it too expensive and didn't buy it. I often think of that coat now. In those days I could have bought three sable coats, had I known there was no reason for saving money. All would be gone."

Monsieur Schébéko was a less attractive figure. There was a steely glint behind his rimless pince-nez which I have since encountered in his Soviet diplomatic successors. He was now employed in some capacity in a real-estate office, but his preoccupation was the preparation of his own memoirs. This must have been a discouraging task, for I recall his telling me how the war could have been prevented. "When I was ambassador in Vienna in August 1914," he said, "I went as usual for the shooting season to our estate in the Ukraine. It was a great pity that I was not in Vienna at the time, for the Austrian foreign minister, Baron von Aehrenthal, was an old friend of mine from the days when he was ambassador in Russia. I still believe that we could have settled matters between us in a satisfactory manner." I sometimes used to wonder how Monsieur Schébéko could sleep at nights when he reflected that millions of lives, revolutions, and the fall of empires could have been prevented but for that shooting season in the Ukraine.

My French lessons with Irina took place in the Kirsanoffs' flat, and there, one morning, we were joined by her nephew Ivan, who had just returned from a night's taxi-driving. He was a stocky young man of about my own age, with a reddish complexion, a broad nose, small eyes, and the look of a Russian peasant. Although superficially Ivan and I had little in common, Irina's hope that we should become friends was fulfilled. We began to see a good deal of each other, going for long walks together, as he said that he needed the exercise after sitting for hours in the taxi, or drinking in cheap little bars of which he knew a wide assortment. He used at first to say that he hesitated to take me to such places, that I must be used to smart restaurants. When I indignantly denied this charge, he added, "I cannot even afford a decent brothel, but must go where the other taxi drivers go." Ivan found it hard to fit together the two parts of his life—at home aristocratic assumptions and pre-Revolutionary memories; on his job the life of a French workingman. The indecision from which he suffered may have had the same origins. He told me that he used to stand for ten minutes outside the tobacconist's, unable to make up his mind whether to buy the "bleu" or the "jaune" cigarettes. Ivan was Irina's favourite nephew, although she was often the butt of his teasing jokes. When she burst out in one of her enthusiasms or told tales of the past, he would assume the sly look of one who mistrusts what is being said to him or is unable to understand it, and he was delighted when she flushed and flashed out at him in a rage. I was soon to find myself the victim of one of his jokes.

His mother, Princess Kirsanoff, had been ill in hospital during the first weeks of my visits to Boulevard Haussmann. Now she had returned, and I was invited one day to lunch with her and the family. She was an intimidating personality with dark, sombre eyes, full of penetrating intelligence, in a pale and haggard face. Ivan had told me before I met her that she liked to be addressed in Russian (the family usually talked in English or French). He taught me a Russian phrase of polite greeting, and when I was introduced to his mother I produced it with some satisfaction. There was a stunned silence around the table and she fastened on me a glance of incredulity. "Where," she asked in level tones, "did you learn that?" "From Ivan," I innocently replied. "Ah," she said dryly, "one of his little jokes and not a very funny one. The words you just used mean 'Old hag, go to hell'."

Despite this unpromising start, Princess Kirsanoff made me welcome. She came of a cultivated and intellectual family who before the Revolution had lived much abroad in Paris and Rome and had known the literary and artistic figures of the period. She herself was a woman of original mind, impatient of shams and affectations of all kinds. Sometimes she could be caustic in criticism, particularly with her sister-in-law, Irina, whom she found a trying companion, although the two women were devoted to each other. I came later to realize that it was Princess Kirsanoff's indomitable courage and will-power that held the family together.

As the weeks and months went by I was a frequent visitor at the Kirsanoffs' and came to be treated almost as a member of the family. Ivan's older brother, Kirill, was a strange creature. He was the only one of the children to have been old enough to be deeply affected by the bloodshed and horrors of the Revolution and the civil war in Russia. He had been an adolescent when the family escaped from the Crimea in 1918 and had suffered at that time a nervous collapse from which he never fully recovered. One could see as in a distorting mirror the distinction of his fine features, and his conversation revealed his knowledge and intelligence, but all was twisted out of the true as though by some nightmare shock. He was a disconcerting companion, with his bitter contempt for commonplace happiness. "When a man is happy he *spits* upon God," he said once, "but when he is miserable he comes grovelling back to Him." Kirill despised the trade by which he earned his living. "When I sell icons to people who buy them to sell them again and know nothing of their meaning, I prostitute my faith."

Very different was his sister, Natasha, a girl of nineteen, to whom I was much attracted. She had a pale, oval face and expressive grey eyes under strongly marked black brows. She had inherited her mother's intellectual tastes and was the only one of the family interested in contemporary books and pictures. She would sit in abstracted silence at the table and then suddenly join in the conversation, making fun of everyone and everything with laughing high spirits. To me she seemed like a girl in a Turgenev novel, with concealed depth of thought and feeling and a merciless instinct for absurdities in people and situations. We became friends, for it soon was clear to me that I could hope for nothing more. She liked to talk to me in a way that she could not talk to her brothers, who shared none of her interests, but I was not the man for her.

In the course of that winter an Oxford friend of mine, Malcolm MacKenzie, came on a visit to Paris. He was a don at one of the small Oxford colleges. Although he was ten years my senior, we had become friends when I was an undergraduate despite his disapproval of the some-what raffish set with whom I then consorted—callow youths who aspired to be dashing men of the world. An Aberdonian Presbyterian by origin, Malcolm was a recognized authority on the life and works of David Hume, the political philosopher. In his spare time he was a devotee of the writings of P. G. Wodehouse. His friendship for me may have been associated with this desire for light relief, for he tended to regard me, quite mistakenly, as a happy hedonist. In politics he was a devout liberal. His boyhood idol had been Asquith, whose wisdom and integrity he preferred to Lloyd George's oratorical and manipulative skills. An active supporter of the League of Nations, he believed that the lasting achievement of the war had been the collapse of the reactionary German, Austro-Hungarian, and Rus-sian empires and the emergence of new democracies in Europe. He was a great admirer of Czechoslovakia and took a particular interest in the newly established Baltic states, which he had visited on a lecture tour under the auspices of the British Council.

Malcolm was a bachelor, then in his mid-thirties, a solid, upright figure, with a look of robust health and well-being. He was somewhat ponderous in manner, and his slowness in speech was accentuated by a slight stammer. He seemed never to have been drawn by any undue urge, emotional or sexual, towards matrimony— or indeed towards any intimate relationship with women. Among his acquaintances there were some who claimed that he was still a virgin; others inevitably suggested that he preferred his own sex, although of this they could produce no evidence. Indeed, at the time I knew him he was beginning to make tentative approaches to some of the women students at his tutorials, but he was hampered in this pursuit by what appeared to be a form of colour-blindness where feminine charms were concerned. He would tell his friends of a "beautiful girl" he had encountered, who turned out upon inspection to be austerely angular and flat-chested, with hair of black wire. These somewhat half-hearted sorties of Malcolm's were indicative of a desire for change. He confided to me that the time was approaching when he would wish to exchange the celibacy of his rooms in college for domesticity in North Oxford. This visit of his to Paris was a further symptom of his restlessness with his present way of life and his desire to enlarge his experience.

Malcolm knew few people in Paris, and I thought it might widen his horizons to be introduced into the Kirsanoff family circle. The experiment worked even better than I had anticipated. At first, though, he was a little discomfited; accustomed to lowering his considered observations into Oxford common-rooms, he was becalmed like a walrus on an ice-floe in the eddies and swirls of Russian conversation. Surprisingly enough, it was the unpredictable Natasha who put him at his ease by asking him questions about life at Oxford. Soon they were talking familiarly together and she was even teasing him about his women students and arguing with him about his liberal views. "If that is what you teach them," she said, "they will never learn the difference between right and wrong." When he got up to leave, he said to her, "I don't despair of making you see reason. Would you give me the pleasure of lunching with me one day?"

"Of course," she replied. "A fascinating girl," he said to me as we walked away together.

The luncheon must have gone well, for it was followed by almost daily meetings between Malcolm and Natasha. I was puzzled by this development. They seemed a most unlikely couple. I could not picture Malcolm as an ardent wooer. I wondered, too, how his Scottish rationalism and P. G. Wodehouse humour could mingle with Natasha's Orthodox religious heritage and her mocking wit. Perhaps she was flattered by the attention of an older man of his academic reputation. He no doubt appealed to the studious side of her character, which was later to make her a distinguished scholar. Perhaps, too, she, who like her mother hated sham and pretension, was touched by the endearing streak of naivety in him. Malcolm, for his part, was embarked on a romantic adventure for the first time in his life. "What," he said to me, "would my colleagues at Oxford think if I brought back a beautiful Russian princess? Quite a surprise for them!" But his romanticism was tempered by his academic standards. "Natasha," he commented, "is exceptionally intelligent. She is at home with general ideas." One day when he and I met in a café, he arrived carrying a parcel under his arm. Unrolling the wrapping, he revealed a view of a French fishing village. Despite the banality of the subject it was a fresh and unusual painting, signed by a young artist whose name was just coming into prominence. "I chose it," he said, "on Natasha's advice." "It will look well in your rooms in college," I said. "Or perhaps better in a more domestic setting," he replied. "You are contemplating marriage?" I asked. He nodded assent.

The friendship between Natasha and Malcolm had not gone unnoticed by her family. Although Princess Kirsanoff guarded a watching silence, Irina was more explicit. "He is your friend," she said to me. "Would he be a suitable husband for Natasha? What are his circumstances? What is his family?" "He has a private income," I assured her. "His family are well-to-do Aberdeen business people." "Yes," she said reflectively, "one sees from his manners that, although not a merchant himself, he comes of the merchant class." Somewhat nettled, I asked, "Would Natasha make a suitable wife for him?" "Ah," she said, "that is difficult to answer. She is young and expects much of life. If he disappointed or bored her she might be unkind. She has a sharp tongue. Also, she is deeply religious. Does he believe in God?" "He is a good man," I replied. "That," said Irina with an air of finality, "is beside the point."

When it was all over, Natasha told me of Malcolm's proposal. "He asked me to marry him over the moules marinière at La Rue's Restaurant. I knew it was coming and tried to stop him. I like him, I respect him, I didn't want to hurt his feelings, but I could never love him. Besides, does he really love me? I find something lacking in his love. It is all in his head."

Malcolm's own reaction to her refusal seemed to bear out Natasha's view. He appeared disappointed rather than heartbroken, and in his disappointment there was a grain of relief. "Perhaps it is all for the best," he said philosophically.

I did not see Malcolm again for several years after his departure from Paris. In the meantime I had learned of his marriage to a lecturer in economics at St. Hilda's. The next time I was in Oxford I went to see them. His wife was a pleasant-looking, sensible woman. They already had one child and she was expecting another. Malcolm was in a cheerful mood and very much the married man. He called my attention to the view of the

French fishing village hanging over the fireplace. "Do you remember the day I bought that picture with Natasha in Paris?" he asked. Then he observed with a satisfied sigh, "That marriage would have been a mistake. Our political views were too different."

Meanwhile, my year in Paris and my lessons with Irina were drawing to a close. She had proved a demanding teacher, with no patience for slackness or sloppy work. I would bring her my notes of the lectures I had attended and the weekly essays I was required to produce and she would go over them with me, line by line. We would then converse in French for an hour together, she doing most of the conversing. My course of lectures dealt with international affairs and diplomacy, and this gave rise to political discussions between Irina and me.

Among the courses that I was following, the one that most interested and impressed me was that given by Professor André Siegfried. His lectures on international affairs paid particular attention to Germany. Talking of the Germans, he prophetically warned that even in the democratic régime of the Weimar Republic, the Germans were already suffering from what he described as "nostalgia for discipline". I quoted this to Irina, who tartly replied that a little discipline would not do the French themselves any harm. She went on to talk about the injustices inflicted on defeated Germany by the Treaty of Versailles, for which she, like so many others, felt the French to be largely responsible. She went on with one of her abrupt transitions to talk of German romantic poetry and her beloved Berchtesgaden. I had always been an admirer, sometimes a blind admirer, of the French, and now I argued the case of French security against potential German aggression. We neither of us could have guessed that the argument between us would so soon be acted out on the world scene; that the Paris where we sat and talked would ten years later be in German hands and that Berchtesgaden would become a name of ill omen.

Princess Kirsanoff appeared less often at table, and when she did she would sit with her hand over her forehead in a weary gesture of weakness. She had become more impatient and irritable. One day, when Irina was expatiating on the talents of one of her pupils, she flashed out at her, "Don't talk like a German governess!" Irina subsided into silence, but in the glance she gave her sister-in-law there was not resentment, only rather frightened concern. I had seen the same look on Natasha's face. It was she who told me the truth. "My mother is impatient because she is in pain, and the doctor says she has only a short time to live."

One cold spring afternoon I called at the Boulevard Haussmann flat to hand in my French essay. Irina was not there and the hall was empty. Through the half-open door I saw Princess Kirsanoff in the sitting-room, crouched in front of the fire. When she saw me she signalled me to join her. At first she was silent, gazing into the fire, then she said, "So you are leaving us soon to go back to Canada. You are one of the fortunate ones. Yours is a young country without a past. Here in Europe there is too much history." "But," I said, "that is what draws me to Europe; its history and civilization." She straightened herself to look me full in the face. "You foolish boy," she said. "Don't you know that the soil of this Europe that you love so much is drenched with blood, that hatred is everywhere in the air? If you had seen what I have seen in Russia in the Revolution—kill,

kill, kill! And soon the killing will begin again." She sank back in her chair, her eyes closed in exhaustion. It was the last time I saw her—she died a few weeks later.

The day before I left Paris, I went to say goodbye to Irina. She was in deep mourning. "What will happen to the family without her?" she said. "I think there are difficult times ahead."

In the years that followed and in the early months of the war, until the German occupation of Paris, I used to hear from Irina from time to time. After that, a curtain of silence descended. When I returned to Paris in 1947 as counsellor in the Canadian Embassy there, I set out to find her. My attempts at first were fruitless. At the flat on Boulevard Haussmann new occupants were installed who had never heard of the Kirsanoffs. The Russian colony seemed dispersed, all my addresses were out of date, no one answered my telephone calls. Stories were current of the fate of the White Russians during the Occupation. While some had wished and worked for an Allied victory, others were said to have been pro-German and were looked upon as collaborators. I remembered Irina's pro-German sympathies and wondered how she had fared and whether she was still alive. Then I thought of the Orthodox Church at which she had been a regular attendant. I inquired after her from a black-bearded young priest, who finally produced her address.

I found her living in a small flat belonging to a much younger Russian woman called Sonya, a devout member of the Orthodox congregation, who looked after Irina like a daughter. Irina herself was now in her eighties and almost completely blind, but she greeted me with her old exuberant affection and seemed hardly changed in appearance. I asked after the family. Kirill had died "tragically". Of Ivan she said, "during the Occupation he was a hero, fighting in the Resistance against the Germans. He was so brave. I was so proud of him. Now he has a good position in an engineering firm in Lille and he is happily married." Natasha too had married, a Russian professor of history—"a very fine fellow", Irina assured me. Through American friends he had found an academic position in New York, where they now lived. Natasha herself had published several monographs on Russian art, which had been highly praised. "Alas," said Irina, "I cannot read her books, my eyesight is so bad. But kind Sonya reads them aloud to me." Involuntarily my thoughts went back to the Russian paintings portrayed on the playing-cards in our games with Irina at the Pension Stucki. Were Vassili Verestchagin and Repnin included in Natasha's monographs?

I was to be reminded even more forcibly of my boyhood days before my visit was over. Sonya had come into the room to join us, bearing a tray laden with a samovar and teacups, which she put on the table before us. Irina began to talk of wartime Paris. I was leaning forward to listen to her when she suddenly rapped out on a note of command, "Take your elbows off the table!"

It was some years later that I had a note from Natasha telling me of Irina's death at the age of ninety. "Aunt Irina has gone," she wrote, "and although I sometimes made fun of her I always loved her, and with her has gone part of my youth." Natasha's words spoke for both of us. What she wrote of Irina and the passing of youth I too felt. Yet there was this difference: Irina was of Natasha's race and family. I was not. I was taken into their lives with true Russian warmth and hospitality; the ebb and flow of Russian talk still sounds in my ears, and I still speak French with a Russian accent.

A BUNCH

OF

WHITE LILIES

*T*HE SCHOOL stood on a hill dominating the surrounding countryside like a fortress, a steep-walled, towered building of dark-red brick dating from mid-Victorian times. When it was founded it must have seemed an outpost of Empire, and the devotion to the British Empire of which Canadians were so proud was still alive in the parents who sent their sons there to be educated. However, by the time I went there in 1921 the vision was fading.

The school was modelled on an English Public School. The prefect system, the cult of cricket, the practice of fagging, the Church of England services in the school chapel still flourished. Most of the masters were English, but all the King's horses and all the King's men couldn't turn Canadian boys into English Public-School boys. When the Headmaster, an elderly clergyman—"old Silver Balls" as we called him—announced that the school was to be "an oasis of monastic seclusion", he got a horse-laugh from the boys. English traditions were like a Sunday suit with a stiff collar—worn for formal occasions and discarded once the masters' backs were turned.

I arrived at the age of fourteen, having, until shortly before, attended a Preparatory School in England.

There, unfortunately for me, I had picked up an English accent. This was a strike against me with the other boys. I talked in the manner of the masters. In the trade union of schoolboys, masters were our natural opponents. What was worse, I was not even a genuine Englishman but a Nova Scotian, and to the sons of the Toronto rich, Nova Scotians were poor relations.

I had all the hallmarks of a school misfit. I was uniformly incompetent at all sports and totally lacking in team spirit. At gym I was such a joke that our instructor, an ex-sergeant-major, used to call out, "Boys, come and watch Ritchie on the parallel bars. It's better than Charlie Chaplin!" I also disgraced the school cadet corps when we were inspected by the Governor General, then the Duke of Devonshire, a wheezy old man with a walrus moustache. Like soldiers of the First World War, we wore puttees on parade. My puttees unwound and became entangled with my ankles while we were presenting arms. These, however, were but trivial matters compared with my failure to be accepted by my fellow schoolboys as one of themselves. I made matters worse by clowning and calling attention to myself, and, as so often happens in such social situations, the more I tried to ingratiate myself, the less I succeeded.

Like all new boys I was on call for fagging duties. Prefects and members of the Sixth Form had fagging privileges. The fag's duties were to act as a sort of valet to his fagmaster: to clean his shoes, press his pants, keep his room clean, and run errands for him. In my case I was lucky—or so at first it seemed. In addition to being a prefect, my fagmaster, Trenholm, was an outstanding cricketer; good-looking in a clean-cut way, he was easy-going and undemanding. All would have been well but for his roommate, Hartshorne, a notorious school bully, at whose approach small boys scattered like minnows.

Hartshorne was an ugly, shambling youth of eighteen, a wall-eyed, bandy-legged, log-witted giant. From the first moment he saw me he took against me. Whenever he encountered me about the school he would greet me with "Bugger off, you little English fart", knocking my glasses askew and scattering my schoolbooks on the floor. Hartshorne was not a prefect and had no legitimate authority over me, but he had little use for legalities, and of all the fagmaster's privileges which he usurped the one he most relished was that of beating. Every time I was summoned to Trenholm's room, Hartshorne was there in wait for me. Beatings by masters were regarded at school much as a painful visit to the dentist, and there was no more grudge felt against the master than against the dentist. Indeed, spectacular ordeals of "six of the best" increased one's prestige and were a subject for both commiseration and boasting. Hartshorne's beatings were different: they were personal.

But it was not a sore bottom that made me hate him. It was his talent for getting me to show off for his benefit. He would make me caper about the room and sing, mimic the masters, and invent stories to amuse him. "Make me laugh," he would say, with a cuff on the ear, and when sometimes he did guffaw, I was servile enough to be pleased. Trenholm was often there while this was going on but did not try to stop it. Hartshorne was the stronger personality of the two, and sometimes I thought Trenholm himself was afraid of him.

Our days were punctuated by the sound of bells: bells to get up in the morning, bells for class, bells for games, bells for bath night (once a week—for the rest of the time we had basins and chamber-pots in the dormitory), and bells for Chapel. Attendance at Chapel was a peaceful interlude away from the clatter of boarding-school life. True, the Headmaster's sermons had to be endured, but they occurred only once a week. It was impossible to listen day after day to the beauty and gravity of the service in the Book of Common Prayer without being moved. We were being exposed to one of the masterpieces of English prose. The obscurities and unfamiliarities of the words and phrases seemed to add mystery to meaning. The rhythms of the language were to echo in one's ears for a lifetime.

The Confirmation Service marked the induction of fourteen-year-old boys into Christian and Anglican manhood. In preparation, we were treated to a talk about sex. We were told that we must not worry about our new-found morning erections. They were an inevitable if undesirable feature of growing up. While sexual desires could not be avoided, when it came to sexual satisfaction it was a different story, for there purity came into the picture. We must clamp down all lustful thoughts and not sully our bodies (meaning masturbation). We must keep pure. For how long was not indicated, presumably until marriage, which for us was a long, long way ahead.

On the morning of our Confirmation the Headmaster's wife made a tour of the dormitories, in her arms a bunch of white lilies, symbols of purity, one of which she presented to each of the boys who was to be confirmed.

Despite the exhortation to eschew lustful thoughts, they continued to breed amongst us adolescents cooped up together, although the sentimental, amorous friendships which are such a feature of English public-school life did not flourish on our soil. We relied on our dreams—and the dreams did not include the School Matron.

The Matron, Miss Melanson, came from Nova Scotia and knew my family. She always welcomed me kindly when I would drop in to see her between classes or in bad weather when games were cancelled. She was a tall woman with an air of authority, middle-aged, although at the time she seemed to me old. She had a wide mouth in an almost colourless face and searching grey eyes that could detect at a glance a boy who was faking symptoms of sickness for a day off in the infirmary. She made her personality felt in the school beyond her matronly duties. The Headmaster himself relied on her in dealing with difficult parents who claimed exceptional treatment for their offspring. Several of the masters, usually the unmarried ones, used to take tea with her in her flat overlooking the school garden. Her most frequent visitor was Mr. Gerhardi, the classics master, a lank, lonely Englishman with a red moustache. It was gossip among the boys that he kept "dirty" French books concealed in his bookcase behind his copies of Aristotle and Plato. Once, when called to his study, I myself found there, in paper covers, books by such authors as Beaudelaire and Stendhal.

When not attending to her matronly duties, Miss Melanson lived on another, more elevated, plane. She was a devout believer, not in conventional religion as practised in the school chapel, but in a whole unseen world of which she had the key; a world of thought transference, interpretation of dreams, transmigration of souls, and astrology. As a caster of horoscopes she could, as she herself said, have been a professional, but she did not care to prostitute her gifts for money. Her horoscopes were for the favoured few, including the Headmaster's wife and Mr. Gerhardi.

I had the proud distinction of being the only boy so

favoured. To what I owed this distinction I do not know, perhaps the Nova Scotian connection. In any case I was deeply impressed by the result. It turned out that, as I was born on the twenty-third of the month, I was what she described as a "Cusp Child", sharing the influences of two zodiacal signs—in my case Virgo and Libra. Under Libra's influence I might do things unthinkable when Virgo had the upper hand. This was all very interesting. I began to see myself as a Jekyll-and-Hyde character. Then it emerged that at my birth Venus had been in the ascendant. This was responsible for the "sensuous", not "sensual" (she insisted on the difference between the two), side of my character.

Miss Melanson's horoscopes were works of art. The text in her neat handwriting was decorated with diagrams of the planets and maps of the stars. Mine was kept in a drawer in her desk, as it would be safer there than in the dormitory.

One late summer afternoon I took advantage of the lull after the day's cricket to consult my horoscope. The sitting-room was empty, but Miss Melanson could not be far away as I heard voices from behind the door that led into her bedroom. I seated myself at her desk and was deep in astral calculations when the bedroom door opened and to my astonishment Trenholm emerged, closely followed by Miss Melanson. His face was flushed, his curly hair tousled, his cricket shirt unbuttoned on his naked chest. At the sight of me he put his fingers to his lips as if to enjoin silence. Miss Melanson, ignoring this gesture, turned to me and said with unwonted sharpness, "You must not come into my sitting-room when I am not here. It interferes with my work." To Trenholm she said in her usual commanding voice, "You must go straight to bed. You have a slight temperature and your throat is inflamed. If you are not better tomorrow, you will have to go to the infirmary."

Back in the dormitory I puzzled over the meaning of this scene. Trenholm's temperature must have come on very quickly. He had been perfectly well when playing cricket an hour before, and why was his temperature taken in Miss Melanson's bedroom when the thermometer was kept in the infirmary? Most mysterious of all was his warning gesture to me. There could be only one explanation, but, no, it was unthinkable. She was the school matron, the maternal guardian of our health and welfare. And she was so old! It was unthinkable, but I began to think it. Nothing had prepared me for this suspicion, yet the very next day it was confirmed when the call for "Fag!" sounded from Trenholm's room.

I found him in the process of changing into his best blue-serge suit. He had leave to go to Toronto for the day. He told me to polish his black shoes and find a pair of socks to match his suit, but he made no reference to the events of the previous afternoon. He had finished dressing, and was applying a touch of brilliantine to his hair, when Hartshorne came into the room. Seeing Trenholm's preparations, he assumed a worldly air. "I guess you are planning to take that cute little Grant girl out," he drawled. Trenholm made no reply but gave a satisfied smirk which must have irritated Hartshorne. "Well, if she knew what you've been up to with Matron, she wouldn't have anything to do with you," he sneered.

"Just because you can't make it with the girls yourself, you ugly bugger," Trenholm shot back.

He must have regretted his words even as he spoke them, for he added, "Come on now, forget it. I was only kidding." But the jibe at Hartshorne's appearance had struck home. "Very, very funny, I *don't think*," he said bitterly. Then, noticing me for the first time, he gave me a resounding clout on the ear. "That will teach you to eavesdrop," he said.

Whether or not it was Hartshorne who spread the story, it was soon whispered all over the school, and as it spread it expanded. It seemed that Trenholm was not the only one of the older boys who had enjoyed sessions with the Matron in her bedroom. How far things had gone on these occasions it was impossible to judge; doubtless tales were embroidered in the telling. As Miss Melanson had pointed out to me, there is a vast difference between the "sensuous" and the "sensual". However, the rumours percolated to the higher regions where the masters dwelt and finally reached the ears of old Silver Balls himself.

Authority was slow to move. The first symptom of change was the absence of the masters from the Matron's tea ceremony. Even Mr. Gerhardi withdrew into his loneliness and the consolations of French literature. Then we learned that Miss Melanson had gone on a "much-needed holiday", and finally that she would not be returning. Her place as Matron was taken by a buxom trained nurse who greeted all symptoms of ill health with, "Take half an Aspirin and count your blessings."

Before Miss Melanson's departure I went to say goodbye to her. "I was born," she said, "under the sign of Sagittarius, the archer. I aim high and seldom fall short of the mark, but Saturn is now in the ascendant, a negative influence for me." I said I would miss her. "Indeed you will," she said. "You are reaching an age when you will be increasingly in need of a woman's refining influence to realize your potential."

Many years were to pass before I saw her again. My family heard that she had gone as a housekeeper-companion to an elderly widowed businessman, somewhere in Northern Ontario. It was during my second year as an undergraduate at Oxford that I received a note in Miss Melanson's flowing hand, informing me that she and "my friend Mr. Sawbridge" were visiting Oxford and inviting me to join them for tea at the Blue Cockatoo in the High Street. There I found them, ensconced in a corner of the teashop.

Miss Melanson seemed unchanged. If anything, her looks had improved with age. Her companion was a heavily built man in his sixties, completely bald; his small, deep-set eyes and prognathous jaw gave him the air of a very tough customer. However, he greeted me cordially enough. "Any friend of Maisie's," he declared, "is a friend of mine." That Miss Melanson should be Maisie was certainly a surprise. Patting her hand affectionately, Mr. Sawbridge said, "I don't know how I would have got on without her. It was her idea that we should take this little holiday together. I have had business problems lately and she thought I needed relaxation." "Yes," she said, "Fred has been through a trying time. He is president of the Sawbridge Mining Company, but there was an attempt to replace him. Negative influences were at work, but they were repulsed." The mention of "negative influences" struck a chord. "Do you remember doing my horoscope when I was at school?" I asked. A faraway look came over her face. "Oh, yes," she said, "I had a sort of craze for that sort of thing in those days, but Fred has quite cured me of all that nonsense, haven't you, my dear?"

Miss Melanson's visit set me thinking. Had I formed a distorted picture of my school-days with myself cast as a hapless victim? Had I created a monster called Hartshorne? For I still could not banish Hartshorne from my memory. What had made him, I asked myself, into a sadistic bully? Was it self-hatred, the rage of Caliban on seeing his face in the glass? In any case I never expected to see that face again.

One day in the 1950s when I was on leave in London from my duties at the Department of External Affairs in Ottawa, I dropped in to Canada House to see our High Commissioner, Norman Robertson. I was told that he was busy with a member of a visiting trade delegation from Canada. While I was waiting, the door leading to his office opened and Norman came out, accompanied by a tall, middle-aged man, who looked like a business executive. He wore horn-rimmed glasses, was clad in a smart double-breasted suit, and sported a small black moustache. Despite these disguises, I recognized Hartshorne at once and he recognized me. He came across the room, hand outstretched. "Why, it's Ritchie!" he exclaimed. "It has been a long time but I would know you anywhere. Those were the days," he continued cheerfully. "Gee, you were a funny little kid. I still remember some of your stories. We had a lot of laughs, didn't we?"

There followed a moment of uneasy silence. He hesitated as though he had something to add, but changed his mind and passed out of the door and out of my life. I had missed the opportunity to settle a score, to remind him of old times with a clout on the ear. I had returned his handshake. I had smiled at his mention of my funny stories. I had betrayed the schoolboy I had been—or had I remained the same schoolboy who was pleased when he used to guffaw at my jokes?

BIMBASH

I FOUND THE LETTER one day when I was on holiday from school. I was rummaging about in an old trunk in the attic of my grandfather's house in Halifax when it slipped out of a package of letters and press clippings labelled "H.K.S.".

Dearest Mamma: God only knows the sorrow I felt when I got Papa's letter at school. It all seems to me like a horrible dream that hangs over my head like a terrible warning that I, in the midst of my youth, will be carried off if I do not make some atonement for my past sins.

I have done everything wrong that it is possible for me to do and being confirmed was almost, if not quite, the worst. I frankly say that this boarding school presents more evil desires to a young boy than you could possibly imagine or that the masters know of or could possibly stop. Although I have improved in my mental powers, spiritually I have gone to the bad ever since I have been here. Anyway, with God's help, I am going to try to reform and lead a new life. I am determined that I will devote myself to the service of God and be a clergyman and to do this I cannot go

back to this school. I am only a child and I am
expressing the thoughts of a child, but I have told the
plain and whole truth and leave it for you to decide
whether I go back to this school and enter the army or
stay away and be a clergyman.

Poor Daisy, whom everyone loved—she seemed too
good for this world—and Fanny, and now Sadie. Now
hoping that God will spare you further sorrow, I
remain, your son Harry.

The letter was dated 1875, and I recognized the
initials; they were those of my mother's older brother,
Harry. But what had caught my attention was the crest
on the writing-paper, the crest of my own boarding-
school. I knew my uncle Harry from the photograph of a
handsome officer in the full-dress uniform of the Gordon
Highlanders, standing with his gauntleted hand on his
sword hilt. What connection could there be between this
bold-faced man and the heart-broken, guilt-ridden
schoolboy who had written that letter? And who were
Daisy, Fanny, and Sadie? I went to my mother for an
explanation.

They were her older sisters, who had died before she
was born, she told me. All three had died in one week of
diphtheria in one of the devastating epidemics of those
days. "Those," she said, pointing to three miniatures on
the wall, "are the three little girls." There they were:
Fanny, with pensive grey eyes, a girl of fifteen; Daisy, a
russet-haired nymphet of twelve; and Sadie, the young-
est, wearing a fur hat and proudly carrying a small fur
muff, a mischievous-looking child with my mother's
dark eyes. Their older brother, Harry, the writer of the
letter, had been away at boarding-school at the time of
the tragedy. As for Harry himself, my mother had

scarcely known him, for he was twenty years older than she. Her parents had idolized him. He had been a gallant soldier and a well-known figure in the fashionable London society of the day, and they were proud of his exploits and decorations and delighted when he married into the aristocracy. "Much as I loved my parents," my mother said, "I must say that they were terrific snobs. I could never forgive Harry for bleeding my father white to pay his endless debts. But all the same, he was an extraordinary man."

"An extraordinary man", yet once he had been a boy at the same school as I, perhaps sleeping in the same dormitory and coming home in the holidays to this house. He and I were of the same blood and family. I could not flatter myself that there was any resemblance between my timid, bespectacled self and the dashing soldier in the photograph, but the writer of that unhappy letter was no stranger to me. How had he emerged from his earlier schoolboy self into the world of adventure and achievement? If he could do it, why couldn't I? Thus began my quest for my uncle Harry, later to be known as Bimbash.

It was a daunting task to trace from the bundle of papers before me the story of a life or to track down the secret of a personality. Harry's handwriting was almost illegible. The yellowing press clippings were falling to pieces with age and jumbled together in no order or sequence. Most of the letters were addressed to his parents, and what man tells the whole story in letters to his parents? Then there were wide gaps in which I could detect the hand of a censor. Perhaps, after his early death, his father, or more probably his mother, had destroyed much that might be damaging to the reputation of their dead son. As for the press clippings, they consisted for the most part of obituary notices that outlined his career and achievements and paid appropriate tribute to the memory of the deceased. But I was not easily discouraged. I would squat for hours on the floor of the dusty attic, reading and rereading the scanty records, looking for clues to the unwritten. Now, after all this time, I find myself returning to the search. In the intervening years I have never been able to exorcise the ghost of my uncle Harry. I have, by a series of coincidences, encountered some of the surviving actors in his life. They have added bits and pieces of memories to enliven or sometimes to distort the story.

Harry King Stewart (he was christened not Henry but Harry) was born in 1861. His father, my grandfather, Colonel Stewart, was not a professional soldier but a colonel in the local militia, although, as the years passed, people forgot the difference and he did not go out of his way to remind them of it. He had inherited a comfortable income from his father and lived on the proceeds. My grandparents were Nova Scotia Colonials, Canadians in name only. London was the centre of their world and they made annual pilgrimages to England. It was not surprising that when they responded to Harry's plea to be taken away from his school in Canada, they sent him to a Public School in England. In his letters home from this school we meet what appears to be a changed personality. Here is a jaunty, self-confident, sometimes insufferably uppish youth, in whom the virus of snobbery is already breeding fast. "There is a new boy at this school," he writes to his father. "He seems a gentlemanly fellow enough and I should not mind giving him a leg up if I knew enough about him. He is very small. Please find out about him for me." (Presumably if the gentlemanliness were suspect, there would be no leg up.) And again, writing about a holiday visit to English friends of his family: "I had a splendid bit of shooting with a whole party of people, some of them great swells, Lord Ilchester among them, and they thought me a good shot for a boy. Please write *immediately* to Col. Medlicote to thank him for his kindness to me. (I know this sounds pretty cheeky.)" He could be cheeky too in writing to his mother. "I don't like the name of Violet at all," he writes about the christening of another new-born and short-lived sister. "I thought only cart horses were called Violet." What is attractive in these letters is the vein of high spirits that runs through them. He had "a jolly fine time" on his holidays, "I had a splendid day on Thursday", "I have now a study of my own at school. You might spare me £3 to put up pictures on the walls." Finally, towards the end of his studies, "Mr. Harper [one of his schoolmasters] thinks I can pass into the army if I work hard." For there was no more thought of Harry's becoming a clergyman. It was to be the army for him, and the army meant of course the British army.

In 1881 Harry, at the age of twenty, was gazetted to the Gordon Highlanders, an appropriate choice for a Scottish Canadian. A year after he had joined it, his regiment was sent to Egypt, where he was to remain for the next five years. A friend who served with him in the army later wrote, "In appearance he was tall and sinewy, with a fine presence and a strong face from out of which shone handsome eyes. He gave the impression at times of an absurdly close resemblance to portraits of Charles the Second. Buoyant and brilliant, he set out with high hopes to carve his way to glory, fame and fortune."

The dispatch of British troops to Egypt had been occasioned by the revolt of Arabi Pasha against the Khedive of Egypt, who ruled under the auspices of the

British and the French, who jointly controlled the Suez Canal. Arabi was an Egyptian nationalist who, like Colonel Nasser in 1956, wanted to rid his country of foreign intervention. In 1882, however, as the London *Times* put it, "Arabi was so complete a challenge to European civilisation that the glove could hardly fail to be taken up." In the campaign that followed, the Highland Brigade, of which the Gordons formed a part, was in the forefront, and it was the Highlanders who stormed the Egyptian redoubt at the final defeat of Arabi. Harry was twice decorated during this campaign, and was chosen to become aide-de-camp to his commanding officer, Sir Redvers Buller.

The revolt of Arabi had synchronized with the rise to power of the Mahdi in the Sudan. When the famous General Gordon, the British Governor General of the Sudan, was isolated in the capital of Khartoum, the Highlanders went with the force dispatched to his rescue—too late, as it transpired. The British were far outnumbered by the Mahdi's troops, and a series of desperate battles ensued. At the battle of Abu Klea the outcome hung in the balance and Harry himself had a narrow escape. One of his fellow officers wrote: "When ten thousand Arabs charged the British square of thirteen hundred men, Stewart's life was saved by a Highlander of his own Company who drove his long bayonet through a gigantic 'fuzzy-wuzzy' who was rushing upon Stewart with his long two-handed sword, even after having received the last two shots remaining in Captain Stewart's heavy revolver." Harry himself, in a letter home, wrote: "The enemy's charge was to my mind very fine and the way they faced fire from our forces and wheeled to the attack of heavy cavalry was one of the prettiest sights in the world. I remember when the smoke cleared our fellows cheered as the Arabs hooked it at last."

After the relief of Khartoum, when the British set about reorganizing the Egyptian army under their own command, Harry was appointed to serve in it with the rank of Bimbash, the Egyptian military title for major. The name was to stick to him for the rest of his life. It seemed that this young officer, still in his twenties, was headed for steady advancement. But there was another side to this bright picture of success. As one who knew him well wrote later: "He was full of generous impulses, sociable and most hospitable. When the greater attraction of active service failed, there came naturally the distractions of society."

These "generous impulses" and "distractions of society" cost money. His chosen friends were in the most fashionable regiments and lived in the most free-spending style. If his friends had polo ponies, why should not he? And who was to pay the bills? Even his generous father was beginning to ask awkward questions. He wrote to the colonel of the regiment to make some inquiries. The colonel wrote back: "I am sorry to hear that young Stewart has been so extravagant, but if so it has been from exuberance of spirits, leading to his giving dinner parties and joining in the extravagance of others. I am certain there is no vice in the lad. He is as frank and open a fellow as you could wish to meet, in fact a general favourite." He felt obliged to add, however, "As to your enquiry whether the expense of living in Egypt is as great as he has represented it to be, I must say that I do not think it is and his present allowance is very handsome and is ample to meet all his expenses." But, as usually happened, Harry won out. His allowance was doubled.

He must, as he put it, "live like a gentleman". His

letters to his father sound the same note over and over again—money and more money; now wheedling, now demanding at pistol point, sometimes appealing to the weak point in his father's armour of defence, his snobbery, by skilfully interlarding the rank and titles of those with whom he felt obliged to keep up. While he paraded his grand friends, he was modest about his military achievements, never mentioning his decorations and writing in the midst of the campaign in the Sudan, "I sent you a letter from Dongola long ago, but in the precarious state of the postal arrangements it probably never reached you as two or three of our mails have been looted and no doubt the Mahdi is now hugely enjoying himself over the inside of the mailbags. I think myself it is rather a good thing as fellows immediately after a fight are rather proud of their own doings and write needlessly to alarm their friends with the terrors they have gone through."

On the termination of the fighting, Harry was posted briefly to Malta. Here his debts seem to have accumulated. Here his demands for money have a frantic note of urgency, and here, too, the censor enters the picture, for his extravagance was not limited to giving dinner parties, and, "frank and open" as he may have seemed to his commanding officer, he was deeply involved in what appears to have been a somewhat discreditable love affair.

Who was Emmy? Was she the wife of a fellow officer or a local girl he had picked up? From allusions in his letters, it is apparent that he had written home to his mother about her and that in some way she had either threatened his good name or made demands upon his purse. Finally there is a brief note from Malta: "It is all arranged between me and Emmy, dearest Mother. I

shall have to marry her I fancy, but do not say anything."
How he extricated himself from Emmy is never revealed,
but escape he did. It was a low ebb in his fortunes but a
solution was in sight.

On February 14, 1887, Harry wrote to his father from
Cairo:

> I am in one of the greatest crises of my whole life, for
> what between fighting illness and that terrible busi-
> ness in Malta and duties and difficulties, changes and
> troubles, I have had a few of them.
>
> You remember my friend, Miss Gertrude Romilly,
> whom I knew in London in 1884, well she turned up
> here on my arrival from Malta. You may imagine the
> result. I therefore put the case before you. If there was
> money enough I would marry her tomorrow. I never
> cared a damn for any other woman in the world. She is
> very much in love with me. She is very handsome but
> I am not going to write any damn rot about her great
> beauty, etc. She is a dear, good girl. I'm awfully
> attached to her. She is a niece of the Duke of Bedford
> and she has a little, I think two or three hundred
> pounds a year herself. Her mother, Lady Elizabeth,
> and her father, Colonel Romilly, are both much
> attached to me. General Stevenson, who commands
> in Egypt, is very anxious for the match and as far as
> interests go it would do me every possible good. Of
> course I know that people cannot marry on nothing at
> all and if you think that it is absolutely and hopelessly
> impossible, write and tell me so at once. To marry I
> must have five hundred pounds ready within the year
> and at least three hundred pounds a year afterwards. I
> am also aware of how hopelessly careless I have been
> about money and that you have every right to refuse

me. On the other hand, it would steady me down and make a respectable being of me and there is no certainty but that she may have money eventually. I consider it well worth trying. Now that I have settled that horrible business in Malta I have no drag upon me.

In all events write at once if you will consent and on what conditions and what exactly you desire me to do. Then write me another letter that I can show, a nice one, not full of terrible recriminations but saying it is absolutely impossible if it is so.

I am still very seedy and liverish but able to do my work. I telegraphed to Mamma for eighty pounds to buy a complete outfit from Surtees of the Grenadiers who is leaving the army. I hope you will stand me this. It takes all my time to live out here.

Please pay a hundred pounds by the 1st April to Cox & Co. to enable me to get comfortably back to London and meet a bill for seventy-five pounds on that date. Even then I shall be overdrawn but this damned illness has put me all over the place.

When Harry, as a schoolboy, had asked his parents to take him away from boarding-school, it was to avoid the evil temptations of the place and to make him fit to lead a new life. Now he was to escape from "that horrible business in Malta" and be made into "a respectable being" by marriage—that is, if his father would pay for it. Of course his father did. His mother and father loved and admired their son. They would have paid in any case, but that his bride was the niece of a duke sugared the pill.

The marriage was solemnized in style. Queen Victoria's daughter, Her Royal Highness Princess Christian, attended. The guests were a rich sampling of the peerage and the higher levels of the military establishment. The gifts ranged from a diamond-and-pearl necklace from the Duke of Bedford to a silver-and-ivory glove-stretcher from a cousin in Nova Scotia. From the bridegroom's father there was, inevitably, a cheque. According to the social correspondent of the *Morning Post*, "the bride, tall and dark, looked handsome and nervous. The bride's going-away costume was a pale grey cloth with white cloth petticoat, trimmed with gold and silver, a grey jacket and a bonnet to match."

Not long after his marriage Harry resigned from the army on grounds of ill health. At the close of the campaign in Egypt he had contracted what was described as "a severe form of fever", and his doctor wrote that "only his splendid constitution pulled him through." There was an additional reason for his resignation. His military career, which had started so brilliantly, seemed to have ground to a halt. There are hints as to the reason. In a fellow officer's words, "In the army success went easily to the 'stayers' who were possessed of guarded tongues; dash and genius for war were handicapped in the running for advancement. It was one of the misfortunes of Stewart to have his really high military capacities obscured in the eyes of others, probably because of a curious personality."

This "curious personality" included a strong streak of irreverence. Though a snob, Harry was never a toady. He did not suffer from a "guarded tongue", and like his sister, my mother, he was a gifted mimic. Perhaps his imitation of a stuffy colonel came home to roost. There may also have been professional jealousy at his rapid early advance. The "stayers" had their revenge. They would teach this young thruster a lesson. Promotion should be delayed.

Harry was not prepared to wait out his term of service

on small pay and garrison duty in the outposts of Empire. Shortly before he resigned, while staying with friends in Scotland, he was presented to Queen Victoria at Balmoral. After a few exchanges on the beauties of the Highland scenery, the Queen put a question to him. "Captain Stewart," she said, "I see by your medals and clasps that you have seen active service. Do you think the army a good profession?" "Excellent, but not for a poor man like me," he replied. The Queen, perhaps not anxious to be drawn into a discussion of Harry's finances, changed the subject. "Your wife is well known to my daughters," she said, "I have often heard of her and of course I know her family." To his father Harry wrote, "I hope, my dear old Governor, that you will not publish this interview in the papers or say that I have been at Balmoral. It isn't considered right and would, as they say in America, mortify me completely."

Harry now determined to try his luck in London. He had many friends there and, since his marriage, some influential ones. It was doubtless through one of these that he was appointed by Lord Salisbury, then Foreign Secretary, as a Queen's Messenger. The job was habitually given to retired officers with the right connections, and carried with it a small salary. The duties consisted of the transportation and safeguarding of the diplomatic bag containing correspondence between the Foreign Office and the embassies abroad. This involved travel in agreeable circumstances. As a Queen's Messenger he was usually asked to stay for a few days as the guest of the ambassadors in the capitals which he visited. It also entailed prolonged absence from London and from his wife.

This from Harry's point of view was an added advantage. Gertrude was a nice, rather stupid woman, who would have made an excellent wife to a conventional English country gentleman. She was by nature loyal and patient, but completely lacking in imagination. He was impatient, restless, and moody. Her friends bored him. They were the kind of people of whom Queen Victoria approved: unostentatiously aristocratic and disapproving of the fashionable set surrounding the Prince of Wales, the set to which Harry gravitated and where he was much in demand, preferably without Gertrude. He was becoming something of a figure in that Edwardian world of smart house parties, where lovers were conveniently accommodated in adjoining rooms, of gambling for high stakes, of shady financiers and royal mistresses.

But such a life cost money, and as time went on, Harry was driven to more and more expedients to keep afloat. Raymond Asquith, whose father later was to become Prime Minister, encountered Harry at this time. Asquith, one of the gifted young men of that generation who were killed in the First World War, was fascinated by Harry's personality.

> Probably the bravest man now alive and certainly the wickedest. If he had stayed in the Egyptian army he would have been Governor-General of the Sudan instead of Kitchener, a peer with a fat income and an Oxford degree, instead of a wandering adventurer eking out a precarious livelihood by trading on the good nature of gullible plutocrats. He acts as a sort of spear-carrier to Lord Burnham, the owner of *The Daily Express*, very much like the condottieri in earlier times. He knocks down people and has his debts paid. He is too beautiful for words, a head like Julius Caesar, and talks well. I have made great friends with him.

Finally this "condottiere" even turned to writing in an attempt to raise money. It was an unexpected choice, and the result was unexpectedly successful, for his first novel turned out to be a best-seller. I have long lost my copy of this work, but I remember my excitement as a boy at discovering it. Already the itch to write was beginning to torment me. Now that I found that he too had stared at the blank page searching for words, I felt closer to him than ever before. If I could never hope to match his exploits as a soldier, perhaps I too could become an author.

Charles Franklyn of the Camel Corps was the name of Harry's novel. It opens with the hero, a young officer, on his knees in the conservatory of a London town-house, pleading his suit to a beautiful girl of wealth and lineage. She swooningly accepts, but with the murmur, "Of course, you must speak to Papa." Papa proves obdurate. "My daughter to marry a penniless subaltern! Off with you!" So off the hero goes to, surprisingly enough, the war in Egypt. Here he leads the Camel Corps to daring exploits. When he returns, decorated for valour, Papa can hold out no longer. "Take my girl," he says, "you have won her on the field of battle." These scenes of the wooing and winning of the heroine were merely a flimsy device to introduce scenes of action in the Egyptian desert, and these make spirited, exciting reading, what the author's contemporaries would have described as "a rattling good yarn".

While his fictional hero and heroine presumably lived happily ever after, in their own lives Harry and Gertrude had come to a parting. The "dear, good girl", as he had once called her, was simply too good for him. She, for her part, finally unable to endure any longer his neglect and his outbursts of irritability, took refuge with an aunt in the south of France. There was never any question of divorce, and long after his death she continued to keep in touch with his family. I myself came to know her when I was in England as an undergraduate at Oxford.

She had by then been a widow for more than twenty years and was living in a flat in South Kensington. Although her husband had left nothing but debts, she seemed comfortably off, thanks, I believe, to an allowance from one of her more affluent relatives. There, among "bits" of good furniture and watercolours of the colonnaded country house of her girlhood, she dwelt, attended by a gorgon of a maid on whom she seemed almost timidly dependent. For there was something a little scatty about my aunt Gertrude, as though she had suffered a shock from which she never totally recovered, perhaps the shock of being married to Bimbash. A tall, large-boned, white-haired old woman, still handsome, she had a simplicity of manner and a lack of genteel fussiness which hinted at her old-fashioned breeding. She was not an invigorating conversationalist, but it was not for her conversation that I dropped in to see her. I was on the track of my uncle Harry.

At first she spoke of Bimbash, as she always called him, on a note of meaningless conventional regret, but I was not to be so easily put off. "What," I asked, "was he like when you first met him?" "Oh," she said, "he was very fascinatin' [she dropped her g's in the Edwardian manner]. He was quite unlike anyone I had known before," and, as if to fend off further questions, she surprisingly added, "He was a wonderful bridge-player, you know. He was one of the first to introduce the game to London. He picked it up in St. Petersburg when he was there as Queen's Messenger."

Only once did she let her guard drop. It was late

afternoon when I found her sitting alone before the fire. She seemed only half awake and to be talking more to herself than to me. "People thought Bimbash was heartless," she said. "That wasn't true. He could be badhearted, but that is a different thing. In the end it became impossible for both of us, but I always loved him." Then, recovering herself, she said briskly, "By the way, would you like to come to play bridge next week? I play with a couple of old friends and we need a fourth."

I accepted with some reluctance. At that time I rather fancied myself at the game, and the prospect of playing family bridge with a trio of elderly people did not appeal to me. When the day arrived, I found myself playing against Aunt Gertrude with an ex-admiral as my partner. It was soon apparent that, whatever the shocks and sorrows she had experienced, they had not affected her bridge game. She played with expertise and bold confidence. When I left the table, I found myself owing her quite a substantial sum. The stakes were higher than I had anticipated and I had not enough money on me to pay. "I'll send you a cheque tomorrow," I said. With a cynical little laugh she replied, "You sound just like Bimbash."

I duly sent my cheque, but the next time I called, the gorgon maid announced firmly, "Mrs. Stewart is unwell and she can see no one." My aunt had signalled that she had had enough of my probing questions, and in her method of doing so had won hands down.

After his parting with his wife, Harry's life seems to have reached a dead end, as he frittered away his time in a nominal job and in amusements which had lost their freshness. From this stagnant existence he was rescued by a return to action. In 1899 the South African war broke out, that long and bloody struggle in which the

might of the British Empire was pitted against the home-
made army of Boer farmers, and in which it seemed at
times on the brink of humiliating defeat. General Sir
Redvers Buller, to whom Harry had acted as aide-de-
camp in Egypt, and who was now in command in Natal,
offered him a commission in the South African Light
Horse. At the same time, the London *Daily Telegraph*
appointed him as one of their war correspondents.
Serving with him in the same regiment was another
young officer who, like him, was both soldier and journalist. Winston Churchill reported to the London *Morning Post*.

Some of Harry's newspaper reports from the South
African war have been preserved. They make vivid and
informative journalism and they strike a personal note.
His voice can be heard, and it is the voice of a happy
man. Gone is the cynicism of the jaded man-about-town.
Harry has again become Bimbash the soldier. In his
account of the battle of Spion Kop he is writing in the
heat of the action, "putting down my pen to march again
with my men". The battle proved a disaster for the
British. The mismanagement of the war in South Africa
was partly due to the hidebound traditionalism of the
British army which Harry had come up against in action
in Egypt. He reports an example from South Africa.

When a body of men crosses an open patch of ground
they are exposed to long-range Boer fire. It is quite
sickening to see the infantry officers exposing themselves at these ranges. It is unnecessary. It is not even
brave. It is simply an idea that an officer should stand
up. Their courage is incontestable, their methods
absurd. I have just seen through my telescope a young
officer standing up to direct his men to shoot, though

[97]

the Boers were hidden from view completely. The poor boy was shot, of course, carried dead past my post as I write.

To the Boers Harry paid a tribute. "I am very struck by the Boers. They are both brave and intelligent. It is some credit to get the best of them. They know where to fight and how to fight, how to retreat and how to advance. They are clever and mobile to a high degree. What a lot they are teaching us, these Dutch farmers. When necessary they are heroes."

One of the lessons that the British finally learned was the necessity to adopt new tactics to meet an enemy who refused to fight according to the old rules. The Boer commando system was a foretaste of present-day guerrilla warfare. It was Lord Kitchener who decided to reply in kind and to organize commando units to "flush out" the Boer guerrillas in a series of raids. In choosing officers to command these flying columns, he selected relatively junior officers for their talent and initiative. One of these was Harry, whom Kitchener had encountered when he commanded in the Sudan. Later, a fellow war correspondent, Bennet Burleigh, wrote of Harry:

> Always judiciously led, his men soon acquired the utmost confidence in their leader. There was no task too desperate, no undertaking too toilsome for him. This is what some of the youngest soldiers have said of him: "May he always lead us. There never was an abler officer." His "rides" deserve the highest praise. He displayed a genius for war.

When the war was finally over, Harry returned to London. For his exploits in South Africa he was created a Companion of the Order of St. Michael and St. George. But as he himself put it, with a typical touch of dramatization, "I am not the former Harry. I am broken in health and fortune." The phrase occurs in a letter to his aunt, a widow in Cheltenham, which goes on, "Please lend me a hundred and fifty pounds *quick* as ever you *possibly* can, as I want it very much. Perhaps you haven't got it. I cannot think that you are very rich but this might save me. Forgive me for asking for I know you love me. Very urgent." When his aunt turned him down, he wrote, "What a trump you are not to be annoyed with me for asking you. You are quite right. I am a very disappointing person. I fear this affair will settle me altogether but perhaps I shall pull through."

What "affair" pushed him to such a point of desperation that he turned as a last resort for money to a widow in Cheltenham? Was it a gambling debt or some dubious financial deal, or an "entanglement" like the one in Malta, or even a threat of blackmail? For now he was deep in the half-world of money-lenders and professional gamblers. Yet at the same period he sent his mother a hymn he had written entitled "Upwards and Onwards", containing the lines:

Still marching onward with a martial tread,
Though steep the hillside and though hard the way,
On to that pasture where our Shepherd led,
Where living waters and bright fountains play.

Was this curious production simply a sop to his mother's religious sentiments, or a survival of his childhood upbringing? After all, he had wanted to be a clergyman.

For his father, Harry produced a treat of a different kind. While in Scotland, he discovered the family's descent from a gallant Jacobite who, after Culloden, escaped to France and served with distinction in the French army. There he married a French actress. He returned in old age to the Highlands, and from there his son emigrated to Nova Scotia. Whether accurate or not, this account of our forebears delighted my grandfather, who to his dying day referred with pride to his Jacobite ancestors and his French great-grandmother. As a boy I was equally taken with this romantic tale, but I have never since attempted to verify it lest it should prove totally unfounded.

Harry was only forty-five when he died in 1907. It so happened that echoes of the final years of his life reached me long afterwards from unexpected sources. When, shortly before the outbreak of war in 1939, I was posted to Canada House in London, I installed myself in a flat in Arlington Street. It was in one of the surviving Georgian houses in the street, and was later destroyed by bombing in the blitz. I had been there for several weeks before it struck me that the address was familiar. Then I remembered why. It was the same house in the same street in which Harry had lived and where he had died. I was to find too that he and I had friends in common, survivors of his day who had lingered into mine.

Among these was Rosa Lewis, the proprietress of the Cavendish Hotel in Jermyn Street, now known to TV viewers as "The Duchess of Duke Street". I had known Rosa on and off since coming to London, sometimes dropping in to have a drink and a gossip with her during the war years when the hotel was still the scene of many odd encounters, social and sexual. She was a very old woman by then, with piled white hair, who often wore a white-braided linen suit which seemed a replica of that worn by Queen Alexandra in a photograph of her on a yachting excursion at Cowes at the turn of the century. I remember that once in Rosa's sitting-room she was surrounded by three or four Guards officers to whom she was holding forth about the Bad Old Days. One very young officer said to her, "You must have known Lord X. He was my father." "That's what you think," Rosa cackled. "You didn't know the second footman at your home. A *very* enterprising young man he was." There was an awkward silence, but she rambled on, unconcerned.

She used often to talk to me about Bimbash as a familiar friend. "He and his wife once stayed together at the Cavendish," she said. "It was not a success. She drove him crazy. He once threw a plate at her. Then later he stayed here by himself. That was very different. He was the best company in the world." Anthony Powell in his book *Messengers of Day* recalls that when he visited Rosa in her extreme old age he was greeted with the words, "Well, you are a ghost of the past," and that she then introduced him around the room with the words, "This is Bimbash Stewart."

Powell was sufficiently intrigued by this confusion of identity to try to find out more about the dead man for whom he had been mistaken. When he mentioned the subject to his friend Lady Diana Cooper, the famous wit and beauty, he was surprised to be told that as a child she had been "madly in love" with Bimbash. I, too, was to become a friend of Diana's, who remained ageless. "Bimbash was a friend of my parents'," she once told me, "and he lived in a flat opposite us in Arlington Street. He used often to come to our house. He was my first love. When I was a girl of twelve he paid me my first compliment. I thought him very romantic. He had such *dash*. My father and all the men used to tell stories of his escapades. They even imitated his clothes, his fur hat and a sort of cape that he wore. He wrote me a farewell letter before he died, and I wore a chain round my neck to remind me to pray for him every night."

Of Harry's last days I heard a somewhat gruesome account from a censorious female cousin of ours. "Your uncle Harry," she recounted, "was living with his mistress at the end. She was *French*," she added, as though that suggested a further depth of depravity. "As he lay dying, she stole all his possessions. Day by day she took more and more until nothing was left but the bed he died in." How she came by this story I never learned. I would not have credited her with enough imagination to invent it. My mother said, "Cousin Etty was a born liar. She hated Harry because he couldn't be bothered with her on her visits to London from Nova Scotia."

The memorial service for Bimbash at St. James's, Piccadilly, was crowded. The list of those attending reads like a compendium of Edwardian society and included King Edward's mistress, Mrs. Keppel. The service was conducted by the Dean of the Chapel Royal. In his tribute he spoke of the "dashing, gallant, and able soldier, distinguished for his unusual fearlessness. He was a fascinating, lovable man, undaunted by reverses, keeping up a brave heart when many would have been downcast." The newspaper account details the occupants of the three carriages which followed the hearse to the cemetery. In the third carriage rode "Colonel Stewart's valet and the nurses who attended him in his last illness". What, one may ask, were they doing when his French mistress was ransacking his flat? The widow was in the first carriage and went to the graveside. Her wreath was inscribed "To Bimbash from his ever-loving wife".

When I was living in London I used sometimes to wish that at a corner of Arlington Street I might run into Bimbash, the "wandering adventurer", and ask him to tell me his own story. But I suspect that he would have had better or worse things to do than to bandy words with one who was not a fellow soldier, not a man-about-town, and not good for a loan, and, what was worse, was one of those tiresome Nova Scotian relatives with whom he could not be bothered. Yet, perhaps once he knew that I was on my way to visit Rosa Lewis at the Cavendish Hotel, we could have gone there arm in arm.

MY
COUSIN
GERALD

I CANNOT REMEMBER a time when I do not remember my cousin Gerald. He was the son of my mother's elder sister Geraldine, a pretty, spirited girl who died at the age of eighteen in giving birth to him. She had married Arthur Branscombe, an officer in the British army, stationed in Halifax, Nova Scotia, who after her death followed his military career in various outposts of the Empire, leaving Gerald to be brought up by his English relations among whom he was shuttled about like a misdirected parcel. An excitable, high-strung child, he was made to feel that it was a bore having him about, and that was the beginning of his becoming himself a bore. Unloved, he was clamorous for attention; unlistened to, he talked incessantly. From India, from Malta, from Mauritius, came admonitory letters from his father. On his visits home he took the boy out to lunch. These were landmarks in Gerald's life. He felt he had a right to love his father. But his father found him a son of whom he could not be proud. Reports from the second-rate Public School to which he had been consigned spoke of his sloppiness and his "inability to stick to anything". Colonel Branscombe detested sloppiness and had always been able to stick to one thing—

himself. He was a balloon of a man, priding himself on being the fattest man in the British army. He had tiny hands and tiny feet encased in immaculately polished boots and his moustache was waxed to a fine point. He had wit and a stock of selfish charm. His military career was moderately successful, but his later years were darkened by a miscalculation. Having commuted his military pension for cash, he married as his second wife a commonplace woman of means whom he counted on to support his old age in comfort. She, for her part, had married him counting on playing the Colonel's Lady. Both were disappointed. Within a year of his marriage he retired from the army. They went to live in Cheltenham, where she kept him on a stringent allowance, barely enough, he complained, to pay for his pre-luncheon pink gin at the club.

Years earlier he had been in love with my mother. It was in the days when it was illegal to marry one's deceased wife's sister. I have seen the poems that he wrote to her, bemoaning this barrier to their union. In fact she never contemplated him as a husband. But she had an indulgent fondness for him. It was at this time, when she was still a young woman, that she was first moved by compassion for Gerald, then an acne-stricken adolescent in awe of his father and unable to please him. Her compassion, laced with irritation, was to last a lifetime. He had just conspicuously failed his entrance examination for Oxford and already showed promise of becoming one of life's casualties. My mother suggested that he might do better in Canada, and Colonel Branscombe welcomed the suggestion with enthusiasm.

From then on, year in and year out, my mother applied her considerable energy and ingenuity to finding jobs for Gerald. As soon as she found him one, he lost it.

There was a touch of the poltergeist about Gerald. When he was roped with fellow members of a surveyors' team in the Rocky Mountains, his foot slipped and he brought his team-mates crashing down after him. Although he escaped harm himself, two of his companions were badly injured. Employed as a post-office letter sorter, he generated chaos. While he was cutting wood on a farm, the blade of his axe flew from the handle and cut the farmer's foot so badly that he had to have his toes amputated. The First World War interrupted Gerald's attempts to earn a living. He at once joined up as a private and served in France. In the army he was looked upon as something between a joke and a regimental mascot. His Colonel admitted to relief when he was invalided out suffering from shell-shock. "A plucky little fellow," he commented, "but no addition to the war effort."

It was on Gerald's return to Nova Scotia after the war that he became, as my mother put it, "part of our lives". A part which my brother and I, then in our teens, could have well dispensed with. He must at this time have been about thirty years old, but seemed of no particular age; rather to be a superannuated schoolboy. He was small and plump, with a perennially red round face and protruding blue eyes. For some reason which baffled and infuriated my mother, his clothes appeared always to be several sizes too large for him, as though bought under the impression that he was a much bigger man than he was. His coat sleeves used to cover his hands nearly to his finger ends.

He was usually intermittently employed, but his real life was lived in the local amateur dramatic society. Since childhood he had had a passion for the stage. It was a passion which unfortunately was not to be requited, for he could never quite bridge the gulf that separates the amateur from the professional. I remember our embarrassment when we used loyally to attend his performances. He specialized in the song-and-dance acts of the period. As Burlington Bertie or as the Colonel of the Knuts, he cavorted before a chorus, twirling a cane, with a silk hat or a boater cocked over one eye.

Gerald used to come to lunch with us on Sundays. It was with sinking hearts that we heard his voice hallooing cheerily in the hall. He always came early, hurrying up the drive to the house and on arrival sweating profusely from his exertions. Torn from our Sunday-morning inertia, we braced ourselves for the encounter. Gerald's conversation was a merciless monologue. Directly we sat down to the table, we would be plunged into the intrigues and counter-intrigues, the outrages and rivalries, of amateur theatricals. "Lola," Gerald said of the lady who directed the local company, "was exceedingly rude about my performance. Of course, it is all jealousy on her part and she knows nothing about the theatre. I felt it would be beneath me to argue with her, so I just snapped my fingers under her nose"—here he mimed the scene, snapping his fingers with an audible crack—"and I walked off the stage." "That was an extremely silly thing to do," my mother remarked. "Oh, no, Aunt Lilian! Cyril didn't think so. Cyril backed me up completely. He thinks my act the best part of the show, and after all, he is almost a professional actor." "I wish," said my mother, "that you would stop hanging about that young man Cyril." Gerald was an inordinately slow eater, whereas my mother was an exceptionally fast one. As lunch stretched on interminably while he talked and masticated she would lose patience and cry, "Do eat up,

Gerald, for goodness' sake." After lunch, my brother and I took turns on alternate Sundays going for a walk with Gerald. It was a trying experience. We were boys at an age when behaviour attracting public attention is particularly mortifying. Gerald had a habit of taking off his hat to any passers-by on the street and addressing a polite "Good afternoon" to them as if he were a public figure; perhaps the Prince of Wales bestowing a greeting on his subjects. The passers-by did not recognize him as the Prince of Wales but they sensed his oddity and his patronage. Some mumbled a mistrustful reply. Others hurried on, casting an irritated look at him. If asked, "Do you know that person?" Gerald would reply, "Many people know me whom I do not know."

We were sometimes tempted to disavow our relationship with him when some boy or girl of our own age who had seen us with him asked, "Who was that funny little man with the English accent?" But my mother would not put up with such weakness. "Blood is thicker than water. Gerald is your cousin and I hope you boys are not so feeble as to pay any attention to what other people say about him. If he had inherited the baronetcy [there was a vague baronetcy in Gerald's family] and was living in a big house, people would say he was mildly eccentric and would be delighted to accept his hospitality. It is just that he can't cope with earning his own living and he doesn't fit in anywhere. Poor Gerald."

Finally, Gerald saved up enough money to go to New York to try his fortunes on the stage. It was only when he had trailed from audition to audition, from hope to disappointment, that he returned home. Something else marked his time in New York, something hinted at but never recounted by him. It was, I think, some sexual

[111]

misadventure; perhaps, as in matters theatrical, he could not distinguish between the amateur and the professional, and was unable to cope with the latter.

Even after his New York disillusionment, Gerald continued to haunt the local theatre in Halifax, hoping for walking-on parts with visiting touring companies. When the romantic actor Sir John Martin Harvey came to town playing in *The Only Way*, the adaptation of Dickens's *A Tale of Two Cities*, Gerald pestered to join the French revolutionary mob, but was instead given the job of raising and letting fall the curtain. My brother and I were in the audience on the opening night. Martin Harvey, in the role of Sydney Carton, was delivering his dying words from the foot of the guillotine: "It is a far, far better thing that I do, than I have ever done." Halfway through his speech, the curtain clattered down, and then, after a pause of a minute or two, was run up again in a halting and unsteady fashion, revealing Martin Harvey looking deeply vexed still at the foot of the guillotine. "It's Gerald again," my brother hissed at me. "I know," I replied.

In the autumn of 1929 my mother went for her annual visit to England, where I was then an undergraduate at Oxford. At the same time, Gerald had come to England to settle his father's estate. For Colonel Branscombe had died of boredom in Cheltenham. His estate consisted mainly of several handsomely bound volumes of Napier's *Peninsular War* (one volume missing), and a monumental silver inkstand inscribed with the names of his old companions in the regiment. There was no money. The widow gave Gerald a sparse welcome. "She did not even offer me a cup of tea. She said that my father had left a letter addressed to me, but that she must have mislaid it when cleaning out his desk, and if she found it, she would send it on to me."

My mother, while in England, was in the habit of having a small sherry party each year for the purpose of "polishing off" some of her acquaintances. More interesting or intimate friends were not included. This was a settling of petty social accounts. That year it took place in the Hyde Park Hotel. The guests had at one time or another served in Halifax, either in the garrison or with the fleet. They were elderly people for the most part, and conversation played over reminiscences of the old days. Sherry was for the ladies and for the gentlemen also, unless they took a firm stand in favour of something stronger, when whisky could be produced from behind a screen. The hotel waiters were dispensed with as my brother and I handed around the drinks. This arrangement made the gathering more informal and, incidentally, cheaper.

The party, if not in full swing, was trundling along quite amiably when Gerald arrived. He had borrowed or hired for the occasion a dark-blue suit which hung in folds about him. On his feet were boots so much too big for him that he appeared to be walking on snowshoes, which he had difficulty in controlling as he crossed the parquet floor of the hotel drawing-room. His manner was eager but agitated. My mother swept him with a look of irritated resignation. "This is my nephew, Gerald," she introduced him. "You remember my sister Geraldine." "Indeed yes," cooed Lady Hoskins, the doyenne of the party. "I knew your dear mother so well. Come sit down beside me." Gerald obeyed and without delay burst into one of his non-stop monologues. His eyes seemed to be almost popping out of his head with excitement at whatever he was telling Lady Hoskins. I glanced at him uneasily. Meanwhile the muted general conversation was continuing when it was arrested by a burst of song, loud and unexpected. Gerald had sprung to his feet and was giving a spirited rendering of one of his favourite numbers:

I'm Burlington Bertie, I rise at ten-thirty,
And saunter along like a toff.
I walk down the Strand with my gloves on my hands,
Then I walk down again with them off.
I've just had a banana with Lady Diana,
I'm Burlington Bertie from Bow.

As he sang, he twirled an imaginary cane, cocked an invisible straw hat, and waved a pair of real gloves which he produced like a conjurer from his pocket. Gaily he capered into the middle of the room. He was not drunk. He had hardly touched his sherry glass. My mother fixed him with a compelling eye. "Gerald," she said. "Would you pass the olives to Mrs. Stormley." Abandoning his act, he quietly proceeded to Mrs. Stormley's side. Major Unwin, an old stalwart, who had rated a whisky, called across the room to him, "I say, what a performance! You should be on the stage." A blush of pleasure reddened Gerald's face, and he cast down his eyes demurely. There was a faint murmur of congratulations from the ladies, who seemed uncertain as to whether or not my mother had planned this divertissement to liven up the party.

A few minutes later there was a rustle of impending departure. Gerald now rose to his feet, yawned in an affected manner, and called out to my mother in a carrying, stagey voice: "Did I tell you, Aunt Lilian, that I caught syphilis last Wednesday." "That is not at all funny," she replied in a controlled voice. "Just sit down, dear." Gerald sat. The roomful of guests had been momentarily shocked into silence, turned to stone where they stood. Then the ladies began to move towards the door, taking leave of my mother with airs of stricken condolence. They made no mention of what they could hardly believe they had heard. Only Major Unwin muttered to me in a farewell aside: "Quite a character, your cousin Gerald."

After the incident at the sherry party, there was a change in Gerald. His ebullience seemed to have subsided. He would fall into long spells of silent gloom, and had taken to talking to himself. My mother rented a house in the country not far from Oxford, and there he came to stay with us for Christmas. On Christmas night we had a small party with crackers, paper hats, and champagne. Gerald sat at the table rolling his eyes apprehensively, and as usual munching his food long after the rest of us had finished. From time to time he made pathetic efforts to simulate gaiety, and once attempted a song. After dinner my brother, dressed up as Father Christmas with a white cotton beard, came into the room to distribute some presents. When he approached him with a parcel in his hand, Gerald backed away from him, gazing in terror at the beard, and covered his face with his hands.

Our neighbours in the country, Lord and Lady C., had been kind enough to say that we could use their park. One day after Christmas, Gerald and I were walking there when I saw approaching us the rather forbidding figure of Lord C., a stout man with a walrus moustache. Suddenly Gerald raced towards him and thrust his arms around the astonished landowner, crying, "Father, Father."

When one has always been used to the company of an eccentric person, one is slow to notice the shift from oddity to insanity. My mother, always protective towards Gerald, was reluctant to face the change in him. Yet, in the following weeks she began to consult mental specialists. They were infuriatingly indecisive about the nature of his illness, whether it was of the mind or of the body or both. All agreed, however, that he had never contracted syphilis. Meanwhile his condition became rapidly worse. He began to hear voices and, in particular, the voice of the Holy Ghost. The mention of the Holy Ghost seemed to decide the specialists that he must be put in an institution. On grounds of his war service, my mother got him admitted to the mental patients' ward of a Canadian Veterans' Hospital near Montreal. He seemed sunk in melancholia. Once he tried to escape from the hospital, getting as far as the local railroad station; but then, having no money and no clear idea of where he wanted to go, he lost heart and returned to the institution. While he was in this wretched state, my mother got a postcard from him on which he had scrawled the words "nil desperandum". She wept when she read this message.

As the months and the years went by, Gerald's condition changed. His delusions persisted, but his spirits revived, and he became talkative again. My mother visited him regularly, and I went to see him from time to time. Our meetings took place in sort of tea pavilion adjoining the mental ward. Always hospitable, Gerald would order three or four pots of tea and the same number of plates of buttered toast for the two of us so that the tea table groaned under the load. After a few polite inquiries about one's own activities, he would turn to the subject of the Holy Ghost, with whom he was still in almost constant communication. On one of my visits he told me with the air of one confiding a cabinet secret that God the Father and the Holy Ghost were much concerned about the behaviour of Jesus Christ.

"They both feel that he is talking too much, making too many speeches. For instance, the Sermon on the Mount, they don't approve of that at all, and they were never consulted. But keep that to yourself."

After tea I said that I must be going, as I had to catch the train back to Montreal. Gerald protested: "Don't think of going so soon. It is such a pleasure to see you. You bring a breath of the outside world." Then, leaning back in his chair, he gazed at the ceiling with a faraway expression on his face, and in a plaintive aside (addressed, I suppose, to the Holy Ghost) he uttered: "Oh, how his visit has taken it out of me; oh, how he tires me!" I hastened to take my departure.

Gerald spent upwards of thirty years in that institution. In the latter part of that time, he ceased hearing voices. His delusions disappeared. My mother suggested that arrangements could be made for him to leave the hospital and live quietly in the country. But he shrank from the idea of facing the outer world again. However, he was well enough to pay short visits to us. He even came to my wedding, clad, as formerly, in a suit much too large for him. I remember a scene in the lobby of the hotel on our way to the wedding reception when my mother, having borrowed some saftey pins from the hotel maid, was pinning up Gerald's trousers so that they no longer completely covered his feet.

The last time I saw Gerald was shortly before his

death. He was lying propped up in a hospital bed in a ward full of other ailing war veterans. He was over seventy by then, a shrunken little old man, crippled with arthritis. His twisted hands lay on the blanket before him. He looked both diminished and dignified. Conversation was difficult, and I fumbled for subjects which might interest him. Of his fellow patients, he said, a shade patronizingly: "They are good fellows, but they *will* groan, which is so tiresome. There is a very decent clergyman who visits here. They seem to find him a comfort. He means well." He spoke with a kind of dry weariness, as though religion was a stimulant of which he had drunk to excess and been cured. I tried the theatre. He still followed news of plays and actors. "Your own songs, Gerald," I ventured in a long pause in the conversation; "you remember?" For a moment a weak flash of his earlier self returned. He tried to straighten up in bed and sang out in a high, thin voice: "I'm Burlington Bertie, I rise at ten-thirty," but then shrugged and desisted. As I was leaving the ward, he called me back to his bedside and said in a lowered voice: "A wonderful woman, your mother."

After Gerald's death, I went to the hospital to thank the nurses who had looked after him in his last illness, especially a French-Canadian nurse of whom he was fond, and who had been kind to him. When I spoke of him, she said: "He was so brave, never a word of complaint, and so polite—si bien élevé."

BILLY

COSTER

N COMING DOWN from Oxford I was, much to my own surprise, awarded a scholarship to proceed to Harvard University. I was blithely unprepared for what awaited me. Imbued with the notion of the superiority of Oxford, I imagined that I would sail effortlessly over Harvard academic hurdles and that I would be warmly welcomed by the hospitable Americans. I was mistaken on both counts. In terms of sheer industry the Harvard Graduate School was more exacting than anything that I had encountered at Oxford. The list of required reading was formidable; lectures were numerous; essays to be submitted were required to be lavishly embellished with footnotes and solidly packed with information. The whole apparatus of scholarship was of a different model from anything to which I had been previously exposed. It had a Germanic thoroughness and solidity which made little allowance for style and distrusted brevity. The product was judged not only by content but by avoirdupois.

I knew no one in Cambridge, Massachusetts. My first social outing was a tea-party given by a professor of history and his wife for visiting Commonwealth graduate students. The professor—a product of Groton and

Harvard—was a youngish man of impeccable distinction, cultivated and modestly self-assured. His charming wife was a companion piece. They carried off the occasion with conscious kindness, like North Oxford academics entertaining American Rhodes Scholars. I mentioned that I came from Nova Scotia. The professor said that his mother had a wonderful cook from Nova Scotia, "quite indispensable". This was my first introduction to the indispensability of Nova Scotians in cultured Bostonian households. "A Nova Scotian maid—so honest and clean". "Our gardener from Nova Scotia—so reliable". I did not relish this relegation to the helot status, the more so as I had grown up in the counter-snobbery of garrison Halifax, where all outside the British Empire, including Americans, were looked upon as a lesser breed.

My place of abode contributed to the gloom of those first months at Harvard. Conant Hall was a graduate residence inhabited by students from all over the United States in pursuit of the Ph.D. which might guarantee them a university teaching post. The stone-paved, brick-walled corridors of Conant Hall echoed with their hurrying footsteps as they tottered back from the Widener Library, stooped under the weight of piles of scholarly works to be consumed, annotated, and regurgitated. At lunch-time, when we gathered to eat a hurried sandwich washed down with coffee from a cardboard cup, the talk was all of grades and courses, the mechanics of a fiercely competitive learning factory. Long into the night, lights burned as we pored over preparations for the next test paper. No revels broke the studious silence, although once an inmate went stir-crazy and hung a contraceptive on the doorknob of the senior student who presided over the decorum of the corridors.

In my own social loneliness and sex starvation, I was driven to work. My subject at Oxford had been nineteenth-century European history, and this I continued at Harvard, but I branched out into political theory, and in the course of doing so became fascinated by the speculations, religious and political, of the thinkers of Cromwellian England. I was drawn to the writings of the Levellers—those daring, sometimes zany, revolutionaries who broke the crust of conventional thinking in their own day. I began to measure out my day's studies with pedantic precision, having ordained that I must devote eight hours each day to work.

The only witness of my heroic struggles was a curious object left behind by some previous inmate of Conant Hall. Painted on the leather back of the chair on which I sat at my desk was the fanciful portrait of a cavalier, his dark locks curled below his plumed hat. He wore a beribboned coat of blue velvet. His mournful painted eyes gazed reproachfully at me if I left my seat to take an unauthorized outing. Sometimes I found myself dreaming of him.

If the cavalier was speechless, my only other companion made up for it. Mrs. Seymour, the cleaning-woman, was a fellow Nova Scotian. A thin, wiry woman, she was a non-stop conversationalist. Her home, before coming to what she referred to as "the Boston states", had been in Stewiacke, Nova Scotia, where my brother and I as children has spent happy holidays on a local farm. This was a bond between us. Indeed, she became a friend, but not an uncritical one. "For mercy's sake!" she would cry. "How can you leave your good clothes lying about on the floor? How were you raised, I wonder!"

I was becoming almost reconciled to my ascetic routine when one evening there was an unexpected knock on my door and Billy Coster erupted into my existence. He had been an acquaintance of mine at Oxford, although moving in an altogether richer and more glamorous set than my own. He now stood in my doorway. Looking round my room with its book-laden desk, he raised his eyebrows in mock amazement—"Quite the industrious apprentice," he said in supercilious tones. "Very admirable, I'm sure. We'll soon put a stop to all that," and he drew from his coat pocket a bottle of whisky. Before the evening was out, I realized that from now on things at Harvard would never again be the same for me.

Billy Coster was an American scion of one of those old Dutch New York families that might have peopled the pages of Henry James or Edith Wharton. He had been brought up by his widowed mother in the Paris of the 1920s, when American expatriates flourished. At Oxford he had at first impressed the academic authorities by his outstanding ability, only to disappoint them by his performance. "If he had wanted to," his Tutor said, "he could have soared over the heads of the other men of his year." But Billy did not choose to soar. He preferred long luncheon parties, drifting hours on the river, conversations, escapades, jokes—all shared in the company of friends who, like himself, treated Oxford as their playground. On leaving Oxford with a fourth-class degree, he came to Harvard to study law, although he appeared to regard the Law and Harvard University with equal distaste.

Billy was wonderful company with his high spirits and his unexpectedness, his self-mockery and his clown-like despairs. A tall figure with a prematurely balding head and keen, glancing eyes behind horn-rimmed spectacles, he strode the streets of Cambridge like one who had landed unexpectedly from another planet and was not well pleased with what he saw about him. He had early announced his intention of sabotaging my academic prospects, and indeed he nearly succeeded. Those were the Prohibition years and Billy introduced me to every speakeasy in Boston.

I still look back with nostalgia to those great institutions where drink seemed twice as potent for being illegal; where a mumbled introduction through a slot in a locked door brought an eye to the keyhole to identify one as a bona fide law-breaker. This atmosphere of conspiracy was highly congenial, although it could turn ugly. Once when Billy was engaged in a discussion with the bartender, he must have carried too far his axiom that "flat contradiction is the only basis for conversation", for the man suddenly gave a signal. Before we had time to turn round, two swarthy Sicilian gangsters, wearing double-breasted suits and satin ties, rose from their seats and, taking us by the arms, pushed and pummelled us off the premises.

One day Billy showed me a telegram he had just received. It read, "Minnie in Manger Friday". "What does it mean?" I asked. "It means," he said, "that my mother, whose name is Minnie—short for Matilda—will be installed at the Manger Hotel in Boston on Friday." "I hope," said Mrs. Coster on the day that I first met her in her hotel suite at the Manger, "that you will be a good influence on Billy and that you will not interrupt him in his studies or encourage him to waste his time drinking in speakeasies like some of his good-for-nothing friends." This version of Billy as an innocent lamb surrounded by wolves seemed to me a touching instance of the illusions mothers can harbour about their offspring.

Mrs. Coster herself was a strikingly handsome woman, with a kind of wild stylishness in her appearance and manner, far from the strait-laced parent suggested by her words. On this occasion she was on her way to a dinner party with some particularly proper Bostonians, decked in sparkling jewels and wearing a long evening dress on which the price tag was conspicuously pinned. "I am going to wear this tag to dinner," she said, "to show what one can buy for twenty-five dollars at a bargain basement." Billy crossed himself and cast his eyes to heaven. "Not another economy campaign!" he said. His mother didn't pursue the subject but, turning to me, said, "Billy says he does not like the Law. It was his uncle who suggested that as a career for him. I never thought it would suit him. Don't you think he has a talent for acting? I think that when I go back to Paris I might ask Sacha Guitry, who is a great friend of mine, to give him a start on the stage." When his mother had departed for dinner, Billy said, "Poor Minnie, she worries about my future. I don't think I have a future."

Mrs. Coster's haphazard projects for Billy were typical of her. She and her son had much in common—the same funniness and the same fecklessness. Billy was a "Rebel without a Cause" long before that phrase was invented. It was enough for him to know where his advantage lay to throw it away, as in the end he threw away everything.

The Costers, despite Mrs. Coster's fits of penny-pinching, were living beyond their means; much depended on Billy's inheritance from his rich elderly uncle. Billy refused to propitiate him. When he visited him he made a point of appearing "drunk and disorderly". His love of shocking people extended to his political views. In later years during the Spanish Civil

War, when most of his friends supported the Republican cause, Billy placed over his mantelpiece a photograph of General Franco. I do not think that he gave a damn about Franco, but he hated what he called "mob opinion". He was a dangerous man to cross swords with in argument, and could demolish an opponent with rapier quickness.

Despite Billy's efforts to prevent my doing so, I managed at the end of my year at Harvard to attain a degree. For his part, he made the mistake of returning to Oxford, pursuing half-heartedly some post-graduate studies there. It was an attempt to recapture the carefree irresponsibility of his youth, and it ended in failure.

In the intervening years, I saw little of Billy, but during the war, when he and I were both in London, we used often to meet. By then he had begun to drink more and more desperately. He lived almost entirely with working-class friends whom he had met at his fire-watching station during the air raids. He invested some money in a small pub in a poor street and used to serve behind the counter himself, displaying for his dart-playing pals the charm that he would not have wasted on the socialites of Newport. He sought solace in the friendship of Milly Lighthouse, a good-natured barmaid. It was not, I think, a love affair, because Billy was a sexual nihilist, not to be confused with a neuter. Though not in the least puritanical, he viewed sex in any form with a kind of scornful impatience. He loathed snobbery and romanticized the workers, thinking them more genuine than his own friends, but he was never quite able to forget that he came of one of the oldest families of Dutch New York.

By the time the war was over he had become a confirmed alcoholic, and in the process a terrible bore. It was pathetic occasionally to see glimpses of his former wit break through the fog of drink. In the end he collapsed entirely and was shipped back to the United States, to die in an alcoholic clinic.

The other day I ran into a florid elderly gentleman whom I took some time to identify as an acquaintance of Oxford days. We spoke of Billy as he had been then, in the sparkle and spirit of his youth, and of the sadness of his end. But Billy had never tolerated sentimentality and as we talked I seemed to hear his mocking laughter.

LOOKING

FOR

A JOB

HAT DO YOU INTEND TO DO?" my mother asked me one day in the summer of 1931.

"Oh, I don't know. I thought I might take in a movie this afternoon."

"I don't mean today," my mother said. "I mean for a livelihood. You can't be a student for the rest of your life. After all, you have had seven years at different universities and the time does come . . ."

"I should like," I said reflectively, "to be an author."

"That's all very well, but you haven't written a book yet, and when you do, how do you know that you can earn enough to keep yourself?"

The conversation took place in London, where my mother was spending some months on her annual visit from Nova Scotia. I had to admit that she had a right to ask the question. She was not a rich woman, and she was still supplying me with an allowance. The Depression had set in, her income was reduced. As a bitter sacrifice she had sold our home in Nova Scotia, only to lose the profits from the sale overnight in the crash of 1929.

"I'll start looking for a job tomorrow," I announced. But what job? I reviewed my qualifications; they did not correspond to any form of employment. It was true that, at Harvard, my essay on Sir John Harington, the seventeenth-century political thinker, had been well received. My studies of the post-war plebiscites in Silesia had been described by the examiners as "solid". I had two half-finished short stories in a drawer in my bedroom and an article on the philosophy of history, which I sent to the *New Statesman and Nation* and which was accompanied by a rejection slip. I could speak French. That was the answer: I would teach French. The next day I presented myself at the portals of Gabbitas and Thring, the agency of schoolmasters' appointments, which had been the last resort of so many of my Oxford contemporaries who had set out with dazzling hopes and had settled for schoolmastering.

I was received by a languid individual wearing an Old School Tie. He sat behind a desk on which filing cards were stacked. "I should tell you from the start," he said, "that positions are very scarce this year. I see from your application that you were at Oxford. What was your degree? First?" "No," I replied, "a Second." "Ah, only a Second. Pity. As to your athletic record, I see no mention of it on your application form." "Well," I said, "I can ride. I did some beagling at Oxford." "Beagling," he said with a weary smile, "an agreeable pastime but not very useful, unless, of course, the school kept a pack of beagles. By the way, what was your Public School?" "I was at school in Canada." "Now that is interesting," he said. "I have found positions for several men at boarding schools in Canada, and of course for the Colonies a Third or Fourth degree would do, but I am afraid the last opening there has just been filled. And as for a Public School in England, I am afraid that as you haven't been to one, you can hardly expect to teach at one. So it would have to be a Preparatory School, and even there the situation is not promising at the moment, but I shall keep your application in mind and be in touch with you if there is an opening."

When I told my mother of this dispiriting interview, she said, "Have you ever thought of journalism? You like writing." I had sometimes thought of journalism. I had imagined myself the Foreign Correspondent of a great newspaper, sending back brilliant reports of experiences and adventures in exotic countries. But how did one get started on such a career? It was too late for me to begin as the office boy who works his way up to editor. My mother considered the matter. "One should always start at the top," she said. "Your uncle Charlie was a friend of Lord Beaverbrook when they both were young. Max Aitken, as he then was, was starting a brokerage business in Halifax. My parents even asked him to our house, although his reputation in those days was rather dubious. Charlie used to stay with him at his house in Surrey on leave during the war, and he said he won a lot of money at bridge off him. I shall write to him today." To my surprise, Lord Beaverbrook replied promptly to my mother's letter, making an appointment for me to see him.

When the day for my meeting with the Press Lord arrived, I was nervous. What could I say to him? What impression would I make on him? I must not be nervously voluble, or tongue-tied. Lord Beaverbrook did not have a reputation for suffering fools gladly. Perhaps a drink would help. I went to the nearest pub and gulped down a whisky. Immediately it occurred to me that if we were in close conversation he would smell the drink on my breath and say to himself, "I don't need an alcoholic on my paper."

[133]

I went into a chemist's and bought myself a bag of peppermints, chewing them on my way across the Green Park to Stornoway, Lord Beaverbrook's residence. It was a large house on the edge of the park. A footman ushered me into a sitting-room furnished in a random manner, as though the occupant had not had time or inclination to make it comfortable. Almost immediately the door of an adjoining room opened and a short man in a rumpled suit shot out, as though propelled from the mouth of a cannon. The mobile features and the famous grin were familiar to me from innumerable photographs and cartoons. He gave me a quick, appraising glance, put his arm on my shoulder, and propelled me across the room to a sofa. Then, in a New Brunswick accent quite untarnished by English gentility, he said, "So you are Charlie's nephew. You don't look a bit like him. He was the best company in the world, and a fine soldier too. Of course he had no business sense, never could settle to anything, but he was a damned good bridge player."

I felt that this was an unpromising heredity for Charlie's nephew looking for a job. "My mother always says," I replied, "that if he had not been killed in the war he would have settled down and made a success of his life."

He laughed. "No, no. Charlie Stewart settle down? Never in this world! Well, you want to be a newspaper man. Why, in God's name?" I began a prepared speech about my taste for writing, my ignorance of journalism, my humble desire to learn. He jumped to his feet, looked at his wristwatch, and said, "All right, report to the *Evening Standard* on Monday morning, and good luck to you."

Before I could thank him he was out of the door. So, with a wave of the wand, I had a job, not on my own merits, but in memory of Uncle Charlie. My mother did not seem unduly surprised at this result. She felt, I think, that Beaverbrook had been fortunate to be a friend of her brother. She herself was now returning to Canada. A lodging had to be found for me in London. We settled on a room and breakfast over a grocer's shop in the King's Road, at £4 per week.

On the following Monday I presented myself at the office of the editor of the *Evening Standard*. The office was approached through a large room where three men were lounging and talking. As I passed I heard one of them say, pointing to a newspaper on the table in front of him, "God dammit, the *Evening News* has got in first with that story about the bank robbery in Stroud."

The editor greeted me with wary politeness. "Lord Beaverbrook spoke to me about you," he said. "I understand you have no journalistic experience. You'll have a lot to learn. Lord Beaverbrook said that you have done some writing. I'd like you to write a short piece for me."

"On what subject?" I asked.

"Oh, it doesn't matter much. For an example, an account of your bus ride to the office this morning, the people, the streets that you passed, any little episode that struck you." He pressed a bell on his desk and one of the men I had seen on my arrival came in. "Now," he said, "I'll hand you over to Jack Forrester. You'll get your reporting jobs from him. You'll be in good hands."

Forrester, a pale, handsome man in his thirties, with smoothly brushed black hair and a world-weary expression, led the way into the outer office. I followed. "So you are a friend of His Lordship's."

"Hardly," I replied. "I never saw him until last week."

Turning to the other two reporters he said, "This is Ritchie, our newest acquisition. He was at Oxford and is a friend of His Lordship's." They shook hands with me and a burly red-headed man with a North Country accent said, "So you were at Oxford. You won't meet many of your college friends here. You'll just have to make the best of us."

I came away from my first encounter with my fellow-workers with a feeling of discouragement. They had made it obvious that they regarded me as a bloody nuisance who had been planted on them at the whim of their employer. I spent most of that night writing my piece for the editor. I modelled my style as closely as possible on that of the *Evening Standard*. Even I could see that the result was a deplorable mishmash. When I handed it to the editor he glanced through it and put it aside without comment. This was the last I ever heard of it.

On my first day in the office I was allotted a place in the corner, where I sat, apparently invisible to my fellows, who came and went from covering stories all over London. The telephone rang incessantly. The type-writer clacked. All was movement and activity, save for my island of inaction, so I started with surprise when, in the early afternoon, Forrester called my name.

"Ritchie," he said, "here's a job for you. It seems some vandals have broken into the cemetery at Golders Green, uprooting tombstones. Anti-Semitism suspected, or possibly necrophilia. Get an angle on it."

"When should I go?" I asked eagerly.

"Pronto, or the *Evening News* will be there first. Take the Underground."

I made for the Underground station. I had never been to Golders Green and I hastily consulted the Underground map to find the departure station. Luckily, a train was just leaving. I squeezed myself into it as the doors were closing and sat glancing nervously at my watch. What if the *Evening News* got there first? The journey seemed interminable. At last I caught sight of the welcome word "Green" on a station sign, and then, beside it, another word "Kensal". My heart sank; it could not be true, but alas, it was. In my haste I had boarded the train not to Golders Green but to Kensal Green. There was nothing for it but to await a return train and start over again.

By the time I finally reached Golders Green, dusk was falling. At one of the gates of the vast cemetery, a stolid policeman stood. "No visitors, no relatives, to this part of the cemetery," he announced forbiddingly, "there's been a bit of an upset here today."

"I am not a relative," I announced proudly. "I am Press. I represent the *Evening Standard*."

"Press," he said. "Press have been and gone an hour ago. Chap said he was *Evening News*, about some story of a grave dug up, or something of that nature."

"Officer," I asked, "what can you yourself tell me of the crime?"

"Search me," he answered. "I only came on duty twenty minutes ago."

"Where," I asked, "is the policeman who was here at the time?"

"My colleague did say as how he was going home for a cup of tea."

I turned away, discouraged, and made for the nearest pub to ponder my next move. Standing at the bar next me was a cheerful-looking man who said, in friendly tones, "Didn't I glimpse you talking to that dumb policeman?"

"Yes," I said. "I was trying to get a story out of him. You see, I am from the *Evening Standard*."

"Well, well," he said, "a fellow slave. I am the *Evening News*. How is your old horror-sheet going these days? As to that story, there's nothing in it. Just a bit of tomfoolery by some drunk."

"Oh," I said with relief. "I had been going to check at the police station."

"Spare yourself the trouble," he said. "Look, I can see you are new at the game. Let me buy you a drink."

The next morning Jack Forrester silently handed me a copy of the *Evening News*. A headline read "Shocking Scene at Cemetery. Graves Desecrated. Mourning Relatives tell of Threatening Letters". "So, the *Evening News* got there first," he said, patting me on the back. "Better luck next time." He shrugged sardonically, and it was plain that he was gratified. I had confirmed his worst suspicions of me.

The "Londoner's Diary" was a distinguishing feature of the *Evening Standard*, an assortment of anecdotes and sketches of personalities. It had a tone of its own, like the talk of a knowledgeable man-about-town. Its editor was Harold Nicolson, diplomat and author. He used to pass through our office with an abstracted air on his way to his sanctum. It was only much later that I learned that he felt as unsuccessful at the *Evening Standard* as I did myself. The "Londoner's Diary" was on a plane far above that of a cub reporter like me, yet it landed me a small success.

One day I had gone into the tailor's to cancel an order for a new suit, which I had reluctantly realized that I could not afford. It was a long-established firm, still in its original premises in Sackville Street. As I was chatting with the tailor I noticed, behind stacked bales of cloths in a dark corner, a large oil painting. I peered at it with a dim sense of recognition. Where had I seen just such nymphs and satyrs disporting themselves in the foreground, with a background of wooded slopes blending into folds of hills under a sky of dark but dazzling blue?

"That picture," I asked, "what is its history?"

"It's been here for more than a hundred years," the tailor replied. "One of our customers in those days was Lord Harleton, a Regency dandy, a friend of Beau Brummell. He prided himself on his waistcoats, spent a mint on clothes. He was a heavy gambler. It's said that one night he gambled away most of his estate. He owed this firm a packet of money that he could not pay, so he left this picture from his collection at Harleton Hall as surety. The debt was never settled, and the picture has been here ever since."

"Has it ever been valued?" I asked.

"Oh no," he replied. "I shouldn't think it's worth anything. It's so . . ." he paused, "old-fashioned."

I rang up a friend of mine from Oxford days, now employed by a well-known firm of art auctioneers, and told him the story. A few days later he asked me to lunch. He was in a great state of excitement. "We had an expert in to look at that picture. He is ninety per cent certain that it is a genuine Poussin. If so, of course, it is worth a fortune." The next day an item appeared in the "Londoner's Diary" mentioning my name and headed "Lost Masterpiece Found in Tailor's Shop". Jack Forrester said to me, "You are going up in the world. You have made the 'Londoner's Diary'."

Soon after, I dropped in to the tailor's to congratulate him, in the hope that he might stand me a free suit as a reward for my contribution. From him I learned that closer inspection of the picture had shown it to be a copy of the original, still at Harleton Hall. I did not think it necessary to reveal this anticlimax to the *Evening Standard*.

My work had settled into a routine of small reporting jobs—fires, burglaries, and accidents. I was learning the trade, and, in the process, finding my way about many odd corners of London and encountering many odd and interesting people. I was also becoming accepted by the other reporters as one of themselves. Jack Forrester had taken me to his favourite pub and revealed to me that, under the pseudonym of Miranda, he was the author of a women's column, which contained advice to the lovelorn and hints on etiquette and domestic science. I was progressing, yet I could not conceal from myself that the progress was slow. So, it was no great surprise to me when the blow fell. The editor had invited me to lunch with him. It was an unprecedented event. I thought that he had forgotten my existence. We lunched at a small, cheap restaurant in the neighbourhood of the office. Over a meagre glass of white wine and a bony bit of fish the editor remarked thoughtfully, "London is a big place." I agreed. He went on, "It's a difficult place to start in journalism. It helps to have some previous experience. I myself started in Birmingham. I have been thinking that you might benefit by a similar experience. I have mentioned this to Lord Beaverbrook and he agrees that a stint in the Provinces would be helpful in the long run. I am sure we can find something for you on one of our papers. I had been thinking of Cardiff." It was a bitter pill, but I smiled bravely. "May I have a day or two to think it over?"

Back in my room in the King's Road I took stock of my situation. Other young men had soared to giddy heights in journalism under Lord Beaverbrook's wing; I had flopped. This talk of "learning in the Provinces" was only a cover for getting rid of me. I lacked some ingredient essential for success in the profession. I was never in the Right Place at the Right Time. I had no Nose for a Story. I pictured myself roaming the streets of Cardiff in search of news, drinking alone in Welsh pubs, returning unbefriended to my lonely lodgings—and an idea struck me. Why Cardiff, when there is Canada? I would go home and begin all over again. What was I doing in England anyway? Canada was my Home, my Native Land. But what should I do when I got there? I pushed that question to the back of my mind. Something would turn up. A week later I was on my way across the Atlantic.

When I look back on my non-career in journalism I still ask myself whether, if I had had the guts to face Cardiff, I might, in the end, have succeeded. I have the nagging sense of a challenge that I failed to meet. I was to spend my working life cushioned by the security of the Public Service. Journalism is an altogether riskier business. Some of my diplomatic colleagues have suffered from fear of the press. This has led them either to a sealed-lips attitude or to outbreaks of indiscretion designed to ingratiate themselves. That I have been spared these afflictions I owe to my stint on the *Evening Standard*. Moreover, I have never been able to rid myself of the suspicion that it takes more to be a successful journalist than to be a successful ambassador.

JULIAN
BARRINGTON

N THE EARLY 1930s, I used from time to time to visit friends in Montreal, staying once with Julian Barrington at his parents' home there. I had first known Julian when we were both students in Paris— he at the Beaux-Arts and I at the École Libre des Sciences Politiques. We had become friends and drinking companions, spending long hours together in the cafés on the Boulevard Saint-Germain. In those days Julian's interests were principally in art, as he intended to become a painter. He was a devotee of Le Corbusier and Picasso and used to reproach me for my bourgeois taste for the Impressionists. I usually came off the loser in these discussions, for he had a strain of the priggish schoolmaster in him. To like the Impressionists was, he suggested, not only bad taste, but somehow morally questionable. Fortunately the schoolmaster was only one side of Julian's personality. In his more relaxed moments, he relished the pleasures that Paris had to offer as much as I did myself.

The occasion of my visit to Julian in Montreal was to be a studio party, at which he promised that I would meet "all the interesting people in town, political and social".

When I arrived at Julian's home, I found him in a state of smouldering resentment against the ironclad conventionality of his family and their circle of wealthy Anglo-Montrealers. Even I, as a visitor, felt oppressed by the claustrophobia of that atmosphere. The house and its inhabitants seemed muffled in money, layer upon layer of it; yet there was no ostentation. Impeccability reigned, and was exemplified in the figure of Julian's mother, Mrs. Barrington, a tall, handsome woman in her fifties, straight as a pillar. I can see her now in the setting of her drawing-room, with its long, gold-fringed curtains matching the mulberry and gold brocade on chairs and sofas. In the background, maids moved decorously. No untoward sound or gesture troubled the scene. If a petal had dropped from one of the flowers in the vases it would have made one start. Mrs. Barrington was gowned for the evening, sheathed in satin, her hair remorselessly marcelled in metallic ridges, as close to her head as a helmet. Her manner to me was polite but unenthusiastic. That I was a friend of Julian's was not any recommendation in her eyes. She seemed to suspect that his friends might include persons undesirable socially—or otherwise. As for Mr. Barrington, his appearances were rare, and he always seemed on the point of disappearing, leaving the impression that he had snatched a few moments from an important meeting to visit his home.

In this, his son was like him, for he could never wait to get out of the family house. He had little difficulty in doing this, for he was much in demand: a wealthy bachelor, and handsome into the bargain. His appearance was certainly striking enough, his looks those of an aristocratic Romantic of the 1840s. His narrow, sculptured face bore an expression at once grave and sardonic, and his success with women was assured from the start.

His manner with them was by turns indulgent and critical, with a flavour of teasing. He did well for himself. With the débutantes he was bohemian, unlike their philistine brothers and fiancés. With the brainy, artistic girls he was the fashionable young man dropping in to see them in immaculate white tie and tails after a ball and surprising them by talking of Freud and Picasso. In short, he relished showing off and having a good time, like the rest of us.

On the first night of my visit he and I were to go after dinner to a party in somebody's studio. Before we left, he produced whisky to put us in the mood for the party, and we sat side by side talking. I soon found that our conversation was falling back into the familiar pattern in which he lectured me for my own good, but this time the lecture was not aesthetic but political. It was at this point that I first realized that since I had seen him last, Julian had become a born-again Marxist. It was not altogether surprising. Others in our generation were moving to the left of the political spectrum. The experience of the Depression, the growing emergence of Fascism, the drama of the Spanish Civil War, all contributed to the trend. In Julian's case, his revolt against the values of his upbringing combined with the pedantic streak in his nature to make him more uncompromising than those of a mildly parlour-pink variety. He began by accusing me of muddled thinking and sentimentality. "You," he said, "will never reach political maturity until you have broken with your family and found an ideology." He had every intention of breaking with his own family and had found his ideology, which was the pure milk of Marxism. Despite his exhortations, I remained unmoved, perhaps from an invincible objection to joining causes or following trends.

As he went on in this vein I began to feel sleepy, a defence mechanism against preaching, dating from my childhood. Julian, no doubt thinking that he had done the best he could for my conversion, removed his tie and collar and adjusted a silk scarf about his open-necked shirt as more appropriate for a studio party, and we set out on foot. It was sub-zero cold outside and the brutal blast of wind coming up the steep slope of Redpath Crescent, combined with the whiskies we had drunk, had a stimulating effect. Once in the street we began to sing "Alouette" at the top of our voices, and by the time we had reached "Je te plumerai la queue" for the third time, we had arrived at our host's doorway. From within came raised voices in strident discussion. The studio was crowded—bodies of assorted sexes reclined on cushions along the wall. I plunked myself down by a tall, bespectacled girl who was introduced as "Sonia from London". Upon my remarking that I had lived in London and looked forward to going back and seeing my friends there, she said, "Oh, how one misses one's friends! I know I shouldn't say this, but the provinciality of Montreal is enough to drive me into the loony bin. If you were in London, who are the people you would choose for really stimulating conversation?"

While I was still pondering her question, she went on. "I'd say Stephen and Cyril. What do *you* think?"

"I don't really know," I mumbled.

"But you *must* know Stephen Spender."

"No," I said. "Of course, I have read some of his poetry."

"But surely," in despairing tones, "at least you know Cyril Connolly?"

"Yes," I admitted, "I do know Cyril Connolly—not

well, but I *do* know him." At this she looked slightly mollified.

The discussion going on around us turned on the civil war in Spain. Although everyone present was pro-Republican, some were for the milder forces of parliamentary democracy, while others struck out boldly for the Communists. A pink, paunchy gentleman wearing rimless glasses was attempting a longer perspective. "When considering the Spanish Thing," he observed, "one must never forget the deep fissures resulting from Spanish history. You cannot understand what is happening in Barcelona today without going back to the suppression of the Catalonian Estates General in the fifteenth century." These words of wisdom went unheeded as the argument swept on. I heard Julian's voice say, "Let's wait to hear what Norman says." This produced a momentary hush of awed anticipation, and at that moment the door opened on a newcomer, middle-aged, flushed, and of convivial appearance. At once, all collected about him like steel filings around a magnet. "Who," I asked Sonia, "is that?" "But it's Norman," she wailed, "you *must* know Norman Bethune." I had indeed heard of him. People had talked to me about his acts of charity as a doctor, his personal fascination, and his revolutionary views. On that evening, however, he refused from the start to talk politics and, demanding some whisky instead of the glasses of red wine which the rest of us were drinking, settled himself down beside the prettiest girl in the room. Julian coming up to me said, "He is not in the mood tonight. It is very disappointing. He could have helped you to understand."

When we got out into the street, Julian suggested our going to a night-club where Texas Guinan, the famous

American night-club singer, was performing. The night-club was packed, mainly with Americans in Montreal to escape the rigours of Prohibition. Julian knew the proprietor, and we got a table on the edge of the stage where Texas herself was belting out songs in a husky voice. A tough-looking dame, she was attired in a gown of crimson sequins and sported a white feather boa. Circling the floor, she came level with our table and, casting the boa around Julian's neck, lassoed him on to the stage. As the spotlight followed them, she took his two hands in hers and, studying them like a palmist, announced in throbbing tones that reached throughout the night-club, "Wonderful hands for a lover." Julian did not appear at all nonplussed by this tribute; giving her a quizzical smile, he disengaged himself, came back to our table, and went on talking about the Spanish Civil War as if nothing had happened. "I have one ambition in life," he said, "and one only—and that is to go to Spain myself and help to defeat those Fascist bastards."

Within months of our conversation in the night-club, Julian had realized his ambition and departed for Spain. There he served not in the Republican armed forces but in an ambulance unit, in which he was reported to have shown great coolness and courage when under fire. Meanwhile he and I had lost touch with each other. No doubt during my visit to him in Montreal he had come to realize that his efforts to convert me to Marxism were a waste of time and had written me off as a hopeless case. I heard of his doings from mutual acquaintances—on his return from Spain he had pursued his painting, which had its enthusiastic admirers but was too much ahead of current taste to be popular. He remained actively interested in politics, never departing far from the Party line.

It was by accident that I ran into him again some years

later on a wintry November day on the street in Ottawa where he was attending an exhibition of pictures. We decided to lunch together. It was very pleasant. Our friendship warmed over a bottle of red wine. Julian had hardly changed at all in appearance. His good looks were of the durable kind. As we talked together I began to feel that it was not only his looks that had remained unchanged. His cynicism, his certitudes, even his jokes, seemed those of a permanent adolescent. I was thus a little taken aback when, towards the end of lunch, he said, "I know you won't mind my saying this to you, Charles, but you seem very young to me, as though you had never completely matured. Perhaps it is because you never broke with your family and found an ideology in which you can believe." He smiled kindly at me as he spoke. I smiled kindly back at him. There was nothing more to be said.

FERTILITY
RITES

I T WAS AT an Ottawa cocktail party some time in the early 1930s that I first saw Betty. I was standing about, glass in hand, talking the usual cocktail-party nonsense, when I saw a girl pausing in the doorway, looking around her with an expression of sly amusement, as though surveying a group of aborigines at their antics. She was extremely pretty, pink and white and golden, with the sheen of youth about her. "Who is she?" I asked. "Oh," said an Ottawa lady in sarcastic tones, "that is Betty Smart. Very intellectual, you know." There were two men with her, one tall, with a long, sardonic, humorous face, the other small and sallow, with a monkeyish look. "And those," pursued the lady, "are her bodyguard, Graham Spry, the socialist, and Donald Buchanan, who has something to do with art." I thought, "I must get to know that girl."

When I went up to Betty to introduce myself, she greeted me with a marked lack of enthusiasm, and there followed a long pause. Then suddenly we began talking as naturally as though we had known each other for years. When she left the party accompanied by Graham Spry, she called back to me, "Come to see us soon at Kingsmere." Her other companion, Donald Buchanan, lingered behind. "If you are free we might have dinner together," he suggested.

During the meal he talked at length about the Smart family. "They are," he said, "the centre of all that is stimulating and interesting in Ottawa, an oasis in the cultural desert." He implied that an invitation to their house at Kingsmere would admit me on probation to this charmed circle, of which he was already an initiate.

The Smart house at Kingsmere outside Ottawa sprawled comfortably on the edge of a lake. After my first visit I came to know it well, escaping there after a day's work, and sometimes staying for weekends. The quiet centre of the Smart household was Betty's father, Russell Smart. Plump, pink-cheeked, and bespectacled, he was by profession a highly successful patent lawyer. He used to say that, when he left his law office, he put all thoughts of business behind him. Not a great talker himself, he enjoyed the play of discussion about him, smiling tolerantly at outrageous opinions but without condescension, for he was one of those older men to whom the young could talk without censoring their sentiments. In contrast and complement to him was his wife. A tall, pretty-faced woman with an engaging warmth of manner, she enlivened the scene with a touch of the dramatic. She expected people to play up and was impatient of slowness of response.

There were three sisters in the family, each attractive and clever, but Betty seemed to me unique, a creature of changing moods and contrasts. She could be gentle and charming, and then could turn disconcertingly to caustic frankness. There was a sensuous softness about her, yet she could change expression as though deliberately willing herself to ugliness, like a face seen in a distorting

[154]

mirror. She was at home with children, and they responded to her fun and warmth. She loved poetry and she knew every wildflower in the woods above Kingsmere. But she was no nature-loving dreamer. She had the stubborn will and intensity of temperament of the writer she was to become.

What was the secret of the attraction that drew such a varied company to the Smart house at Kingsmere? For a varied company we were. There were broadcasters and civil servants, aspiring politicians and journalists, would-be writers and artists, young aides-de-camp from Government House in Ottawa, and the more spirited members of the diplomatic corps. They came and went, declaimed and joked and argued. Many of them ended up in love with one of the sisters, sometimes with all three, simultaneously or in succession.

What did we talk about on those long summer evenings on that screened-in verandah over the lake? There was a sense of release in the air, release from the tight small-town values that governed the Ottawa of those days, for Ottawa, beneath its political superstructure and its social aspirations, was still a Canadian small town. Here at Kingsmere unorthodox opinions flourished. We could discuss books that shocked, pictures that were criticized, politics that were disapproved. We spoke too of our hopes for a different Canada, of the need for new ideas to break the crust of conventional thinking and of sterile party politics. Then we would turn to ridiculing the notions of social and sexual respectability, for respectability, now somewhat dented, was then securely entrenched. It was not so much a moral or a religious attitude as it had been in Victorian times, but rather a matter of playing safe, like investing in risk-free securities. For young men with their careers to make, for girls brought up for marriage, any deviation lowered the value of the investment—that is, if it was found out.

Our gatherings were not solemn seminars. People came from sheer sociability and for the schemes for amusement that always seemed to be afoot and of which Betty was often the instigator. The fertility rite was an inspiration of hers.

The exact nature of this festival was in doubt. Descriptions of ancient fertility rites included the spilling of semen to fecundate the furrows, but this we agreed would be pushing things a bit too far. We must all do what the inspiration of the moment suggested, yet some choreography was needed. There must be a ritual dance, a sacred fire, music, and the chanting of runic spells. It was decided that the company invited should not be limited to our own group. Everyone should select guests on whom his or her fancy lighted. There were to be no restrictions of age or compatability. This was to be no congenial social gathering but a pagan festival.

Then there was the question of finding a site for our revels. On a nearby hill stood a group of stone ruins which the prime minister, Mackenzie King, had assembled around his country house at Kingsmere. They reflected the whims and manias of the extraordinary man who brought them together, ranging as they did from a gaping window embrasure from a defunct Ottawa bank to cloisters and pseudo-Corinthian Greek columns. This was to be the backdrop for the rites; costume was left to individuals to decide. Food and drink were important considerations. Someone asked Betty what we would drink, and I was appalled to hear her say, "Why, mead, of course, like the Anglo-Saxons. It's easy to make. You take honey, add beer, and flavour it with aromatic spirits." I privately planned to take along a flask of whisky.

The hour chosen was to be at the setting of the sun. It was a cool spring night when the company, numbering from twenty to thirty, were to assemble at the hilltop, where a circle of loose stones had been laid in a grassy clearing, and a bonfire had been lit. By the time I arrived, I could discern by the fading light a strange and motley collection of figures straggling up the hill, some laden with hampers of food, others with bottles in their hands. Choice of costume had run riot. Nymphs and satyrs mingled with Druids. I myself had decided on a kind of knee-length shift, fashioned from cheesecloth and decidedly chilly around the flanks. Round my head I wore a wreath of ivy, intended to be Bacchanalian. An elderly lady known for her love affairs in remote Edwardian days had elected to appear as an abbess. A starched white coif outlined her wine-flushed face. Trailing her habiliments behind her, she looked on her way not to a pagan festival but to a black mass. From Government House came a tall, stiff Guards officer, with a strawberry complexion and a neatly brushed grey moustache. On arrival he divested himself of his immaculate double-breasted suit and stood forth in long woollen underwear, over which he draped a tiger-skin rug borrowed from the hall of Government House. He grasped in his hand an assegai, suggesting a Zulu chieftain. Some of the guests had fortified themselves for the occasion, and arrived in roaring spirits. Betty insisted that all must partake of the mead, and a witches' brew it proved to be, for to the honey and beer nameless potions had been added. Among them I could detect a strong whiff of rye whisky.

Music was provided by a gramophone which played alternately either "L'après-midi d'un faune" or Ravel's

"Bolero", and hand in hand to its scratchy tones we trod the measures of a ritual dance, stumbling and lurching to the hypnotic whine of the "Bolero" or breaking ranks to give individual interpretations of the faun. Betty herself mimed a series of roles, now a shy nymph, now a pursuing maenad. It was a moonless night, and by the flickering rays of the bonfire the mock ruins around us looked like a grotesque stage set. We were glad of the warmth of the bonfire, for a stiff breeze had sprung up and blew sharply over the exposed hilltop. We were grateful, too, for the bottles of red wine which some of the guests had brought with them, but the mixture with the mead was phenomenally intoxicating. "Now," the cry went up, "it's time for the fertility rites." Some couples staggered towards the surrounding bushes, from which bursts of laughter could be heard. As the bonfire sank to its embers, the stricken field was littered with the recumbent bodies of promising civil servants, aspiring diplomats, ornaments of the Bank of Canada, and the flower of Ottawa's young-womanhood. There was no sign of Betty. The Circe who by her spells had reduced us to this sorry state had vanished. The abbess was gone, flown off perhaps on a broomstick. The Zulu chieftain had departed with his assegai. At dawn the survivors retired to the Smarts' house for eggs and bacon before returning to the workaday world.

Betty soon became less carefree and more impatient with the Ottawa social round. She had no intention of fitting into this existence. She was indeed on the brink of the complete break with her family and with her previous life, which in the end was spurred by a romantic passion. But perhaps at another level the potential writer in her felt the need for deepening experience to bring her gift to the surface. Of the drama that followed, Betty herself has written in *By Grand Central Station I Sat Down and Wept.*

The Smarts have long left Kingsmere. The survivors of the company that gathered there in their youth are old men and women. Betty herself is dead.

One autumn day some years ago, I found myself in the neighbourhood of the Smarts' former house, and on impulse decided to pay it a visit, though I reflected that the Betty I had known and loved would have had no use for mooning about the ruins of her old home. That was not at all her style.

The house had long since been sold and resold. The paths approaching it were thick with dead leaves; the lattice woodwork of the verandah had warped and rotted; there was an odd tilt to the sloping roof. The very foundations seemed on the point of slithering, yet through the windows one could see furniture within. People, if they did not live there, visited or camped there. When I turned the handle, the front door opened into the dank stillness of the empty room. Armchairs and bulky tables were set about clumsily. There were empty beer cans on the floor, a dismembered sofa was disintegrating in a corner. The rooms seemed reduced in size. Had their actual proportions changed? That seemed impossible, but surely the gallery room with its window seats where we used to sit overlooking the lake had been longer? Where had we all stood, moved, and talked on those long summer evenings? The questions seemed hardly worth asking. This was a dead page of the past; it housed no ghosts and held no echoes. It touched no nerve of nostalgia.

RUMOURS

OF

WAR

LITTLE DID I THINK when my year at Harvard was completed that I should ever return there, but three years later I did so. Harvard awarded me a further scholarship and a second chance to prove myself a serious historian. This time there was no Billy Coster, and this time I had found a topic which engrossed me. My thesis for a Ph.D. dealt with the origins of the First World War. It was an ambitious project, involving the study of diplomatic documents—telegrams, dispatches, and memoranda of the period, in English, French, and German. This was history in the making, before it had congealed into the historian's retrospective narrative of cause and effect. It was the record, couched in diplomatic language, of one of the most disastrous failures of diplomacy in history— the failure to prevent a world war which no one wanted. The actors in this drama seemed to drift helplessly towards the abyss, blind to the forces which would sweep so many of them into oblivion. In the face of such lack of vision, it seemed idle to indulge in the game of "Who was to blame?" Was it the unstable, vainglorious German emperor William II, a puppet self-condemned to play the part of warlord; or the Russian Empire, bankrupt of hope, entering the war fatalistically; or the French, obsessed with revenge for humiliations at German hands; or the British, who muddled their way into the trap; or the Austrians, who precipitated the outcome by their frivolity and overbearingness? When it came to war guilt, it seemed to this student that one could only fall back on the doctrine of Original Sin.

Professional diplomats did not figure among the warmongers. Some strove to avert the catastrophe, but they were servants of their masters, the emperors and the politicians. It was a useful lesson for a future member of their profession. The diplomat functions within limitations. He may try to serve humanity while serving the interests of his country, but what if these do not coincide? He can of course resign. In practice few diplomats do.

As I followed the day-to-day pattern of negotiations, ultimatums, and mobilizations in that month of July 1914, I could not have foreseen those days in the summer of 1939 when, as a Foreign Service Officer at Canada House in London, I made daily visits to the Foreign Office, there to receive for transmission to Ottawa the diplomatic telegrams outlining the negotiations, ultimatums, and mobilizations leading up to the outbreak of the Second World War. If these were the lessons of history, they were not encouraging. Perhaps they accounted for the sceptical frame of mind in which I came to regard schemes for making the world a better place, preferring the more modest aim of preventing it from becoming a much worse one.

As it turned out, my thesis on the origins of the First World War was never completed. Before it was finished, an announcement appeared of examinations for Third Secretaries in the Canadian Department of External

Affairs. I applied at once. By special arrangement, Canadians living abroad could compete in the country where they found themselves. In Boston the examinations were held in the State Capitol. It was blazingly hot August weather. The sun burnished the dome of the capitol building. Inside, solemn-faced officials broke the seals of the envelopes sent from Ottawa containing the examination papers. There were a handful of examinees, mostly graduate students like myself. The examination papers included an essay question for which several alternative choices were indicated. I hastily averted my eyes from "The Fishery Problems of the North Pacific" and "Trade Relations with the United States" in favour of "Canada's Contribution to the League of Nations".

A long and anxious waiting period ensued before a summons to appear before a Board of the Department in Ottawa indicated that I had passed the written examination. The Board was composed of departmental officials, headed by the Under-Secretary of State for External Affairs, Dr. O. D. Skelton, who, ignoring my essay on the League of Nations, asked me a question relating to the North Pacific fisheries. I gazed at him in dumb dismay and he mercifully let the subject drop. I was luckier in my encounter with the Assistant Under-Secretary, Laurent Beaudry, a French Canadian with whom I was able to converse in French, thus scoring off the other examinees, few of whom had ever attempted that language. Sitting at the end of the table, the most junior of the examiners was a boyish-looking man in a crumpled suit, whom I did not spot as a future prime minister and a Nobel Prize winner—Mike Pearson.

Despite my ignorance of the North Pacific fisheries, I was accepted by the Examining Board. I had now got over the first two hurdles, the written and the oral examinations, but there remained the most formidable obstacle on the course—the interview with the Prime Minister, the Right Honourable Richard Bedford Bennett. In those days the Prime Minister doubled as Secretary of State for External Affairs, and Mr. Bennett made it a point to interview all candidates for the Department of External Affairs.

It was a nervous gaggle of candidates who presented themselves in the Prime Minister's enormous Victorian Gothic office in the East Block of the Parliament Buildings. Mr. Bennett was himself a man of large displacement, as they say of ocean liners; massively stout, he was of rubicund complexion, and his triple chins were encased in an old-fashioned wing collar. The Prime Minister greeted us with almost alarming joviality, chuckling and rubbing his hands together. He addressed to each of us a few brief remarks and questions. It became clear that he was fully acquainted with our examination records but wanted to form his own impressions of our suitability by the mysterious chemistry known to politicians. Having no doubt reached his own conclusions, he dismissed us with a homily. "I know," he said, "that each of you young men hopes to be accepted into the public service of your country and to have the privilege of serving Canada, but you must remember that while many are called few are chosen." On this rather ominous note we departed. As it turned out, I proved to be one of the chosen few. My long-drawn-out academic education had ended. What lay ahead was education of a different kind.

Envoi

ONE SUNNY DAY last summer I was standing on the wharf in Chester, Nova Scotia, gazing out to sea, thinking about the dead people of whom I had been writing and of the changing scenes of my own life. I was shaken out of these Proustian musings by a hand grabbing my arm. It was an old fisherman whom I had often encountered on the wharf. Today he seemed slightly the worse for drink.

"How are you doing, old stick?" he inquired.

"Fine," I replied.

I went on my way in a more cheerful mood. The encounter had brought me down to earth, the earth of my native Nova Scotia, where it had all begun.